THE
Fine Art of
HOSPITALITY

THE *Fine Art of* HOSPITALITY

Sharing Your
Heart & Home
With Others

Edited by Sheila Jones
Foreword by Wyndham Shaw

DPI
DISCIPLESHIP
PUBLICATIONS
INTERNATIONAL

One Merrill Street
Woburn, MA 01801
1 (800) 727-8273 FAX (617) 937-3889

The Fine Art of Hospitality
©1995 by Discipleship Publications International
One Merrill Street, Woburn, MA 01801

Book design and interior illustrations by Chris Costello
Cover art by Chris Costello

Printed in the United States of America

ISBN 1-884553-65-6

CONTENTS

Practice Hospitality

The Lost Art of Hospitality could easily be a book title describing the lives of most people in our world today. A drastic decline in hospitality, inviting others into the privacy and warmth of our homes, has occurred in my lifetime. Busy schedules, selfish hearts and material possessions have replaced the practice of hospitality with the pursuit of personal gain. We use people and love things rather than using things to love people.

Hospitality is not only a fine art, but a command of God, a need of people everywhere, and a joy that brings many blessings to those who practice it. I grew up in a family of ten in the southern United States. We did not have a lot of money, but we always had plenty of good food, a cheery fire and lots of fun conversation for all who came to visit the Shaws. My mother's philosophy was, "There's always room for one more" either for dinner or overnight at the "Shaw Motel." Sunday dinner always found at least one or more of our friends at the long dining room table. Roast beef, mashed potatoes and gravy, homemade rolls and a happy family atmosphere always created the desire for a return visit. I was happy to have a permanent seat at that table!

As an elder and a disciple of twenty-three years, my appreciation for those boyhood experiences has deepened. I now see how I must take what I have learned and expand on it to fulfill God's plan for me as a disciple. We all need to realize that people around us are starving for attention, affection and love. They do not care about how much we know until they know how much we care.

The needs and opportunities for hospitality are myriad. For example, my wife and I are pursuing the adoption of two Romanian orphans as this book goes to press. And our invitations to others to attend church services with us should also include invitations into our homes. I'll never forget being invited out to lunch after my first visit to church. It told me these people were different because they hardly knew me, but still shared their lives with me!

As people study the Bible, they need to see and feel the

realness of our faith through the hospitality of our homes and family. New Christians will only become "old" Christians if they become attached to the heart of fellowship through our hospitality. A survey of older Christians who had nearly fallen away at different times, revealed that most credit both time and talks in Christian homes as the key to bringing them through their troubled times. All of the above represent ways that disciples can and need to bring others into their lives and families as we practice hospitality.

The Fine Art of Hospitality is convicting, inspiring and practical for old and new disciples alike. Sheila Jones is to be commended for focusing our attention on such a vital need for the evangelizing, shepherding and Christ-like character of us all. She and her family are great examples of what the book is all about. My prayer and charge is that we all become God's experts in the fine art of hospitality as we share his love.

Wyndham Shaw
Boston, Mass.
August 1995

Restorers of the Lost Art

Many people have a difficult time relating to the word "hospitality." To Generation Xers it conjures up pictures of prim and proper fifty-something ladies in white gloves eating finger sandwiches and petits fours—accompanied by classical music and inane conversation. Many, if not most, have a skewed view of hospitality and feel awkward in their attempts to practice it. Some grew up in homes where their parents rarely, if ever, invited non-relatives to eat a meal. Others watched from a safe distance as their mothers fretted and fumed over a meal as if their total worth as a person depended upon the impression made on the guests that evening. Still others remember fathers who were anything but enthusiastic that they would be required to leave the TV set, and accompanying TV tray, to sit at the table and talk to people they didn't know and didn't *care* to know. Another scenario is an evening of entertaining which took weeks to plan, exhaustion to execute, and months to recover from. Little wonder that the meaning of hospitality got lost somewhere between the tension and tiredness, between the clean towels in the bathroom and the menacing look from Mom when you sneezed at the table without "covering."

The Scriptures are clear. We are commanded to "practice hospitality" (Romans 12:13). For those of us who are followers of Jesus and of his Word, we must know what hospitality is so we can be obedient and *practice* it. The Jewish people in biblical times placed the highest priority upon being hospitable to others—especially strangers. During feast time, homes in Jerusalem and surrounding towns were opened to pilgrims coming to the Holy City to worship at the temple. There were no Holiday Inns, no McDonald's, no RV camps with electricity hookups and hot showers. They relied upon each other for food and shelter when they were away from home.

Hospitality, simply defined, is sharing your heart and your home with others. A truly hospitable person is a giver, a person with a servant heart. He or she is sensitive to the needs of others and is willing and eager to expend energy, time and money to meet those needs. With this heart, they welcome others into a home in which they already show hospitality to their own family. Hospitality is not necessarily elegant entertaining; it is not rising to the occasion to put on a good show; it is not a cloak to dress up in and take off after guests leave. It is a reflection of the very heart of God to others. He gave the best he had, freely and ungrudgingly, to meet our most basic need. He measures our gratitude by the way we, in turn, meet the needs of others. In the well-known passage about the separation of the sheep from the goats, Jesus says:

> *Then the king will say to those on his right, "Come, you who are blessed by my Father; take your inheritance, the kingdom prepared for you since the creation of the world. For I was hungry and you gave me something to eat, I was thirsty and you gave me something to drink, I was a stranger and you invited me in, I needed clothes and you clothed me, I was sick and you looked after me, I was in prison and you came to visit me" (Matthew 25:34-36).*

Hospitality is not just a good thing to do if you are so inclined by talent and background. It is a matter of our relationship with God; Jesus says it has a direct correlation to our salvation.

The purpose of this book is to clearly and biblically define this elusive word. It is to put flesh on the skeletal understanding that even many mature Christians have. Hospitality is truly a lost art in the '90s—the age of convenience food, two-working-parent and single-parent households, and comfortable isolation. People need not only a working definition of hospitality and an accompanying heart change, they need help—practical, get-down-to-it, brass-tacks instruction. *The Fine Art of Hospitality* will go to the center of this lost art and capture its essence through instruction, example and honest confession. The writers are committed to practicing hospitality. They follow Jesus and reflect his heart in their lives. They are not yet perfect in their practice, but every one of them in one way or another is exemplary.

In order to be encouraging and effective in our hospitality, we must be content in the situations (houses or apartments) God has given us. We must have order and consistency in cleaning and decorating our houses, so we can reflect the nature and beauty of God's character. The first section of the book is entitled simply "House" and will give you both inspiration and direction in managing your household.

The second section, entitled "Home," takes it a step further: You can have a beautiful house and well-organized approaches to maintaining it, but you can miss the whole meaning of "home" as God intended it. Home is the heart of hospitality. Building warmth and trust within your own family is essential to inviting others to join you as family. Home should be a safe harbor for children and guests alike. Even if you live in a singles' household (or by yourself), you can and must foster a sense of home and family.

After setting your house in order and establishing family in your home, you are ready to learn more about the meaning and practice of hospitality itself. In section three, entitled "Hospitality," you will discover both biblical commands for and biblical examples of hospitality. Sharing your food and home with those who are not disciples is one of the best ways to show them your heart and life; it is also one of the best ways to encourage those who are already disciples. Peter says to disciples, "Offer hospitality to one another without grumbling" (1 Peter 4:9). There is something disarming and vulnerable about inviting others into your home. As you show hospitality, they will see the love of God.

Through the experiences and confessions of the writers, you can check the attitudes of your own heart and learn to be a willing, humble, grateful and fun-loving giver.

The companion spiral-bound volume, *The Fine Art of Hospitality Handbook,* is divided into two sections: (1) practical tips to better equip you to practice hospitality and (2) recipes for all occasions. It is designed to be a constant kitchen companion—the type of companion that weathers milk spills, egg plops, flour dustings and becomes dearer with the happy mess of the hospitality process.

A giving of what you have to others. Hospitality. The Bible commands it. Even without an earthly home, Jesus lived it. He showed his heart of hospitality as he told his disciples, "In my Father's house are many rooms; if it were not so, I would have told you. I am going there to prepare a place for you" (John 14:2). He showed it as he prepared a meal of fish and bread on the shore of the lake after his resurrection. The Lord of the universe said simply, "Come and have breakfast" (John 21:12). And as we respond to his example and his command, opening our lives and our homes to others with a joyful and unconditional love, we will come to know the heart of the one we yearn so much to imitate. We will reflect his heart to others, and they will grow in the warmth of that reflection.

Sheila Jones
June 1995

Part I

·HOUSE·

The wise woman builds her house,
but with her own hands the foolish one
tears hers down.

PROVERBS 14:1

CHAPTER 1

Content, but Not Complacent

THERESA FERGUSON

Jesus had a heart to meet the needs of people. He emptied himself to give us all we need. He became poor to make us rich, and by this, he taught us the meaning of hospitality: a giving of yourself to others.

In response to one who wanted to follow him Jesus said, "Foxes have holes and birds of the air have nests, but the Son of Man has no place to lay his head" (Luke 9:58). Jesus was content with what he had; he was not dependent on anything physical. Yet, without possessions (much less *nice* ones), he was able to influence people and change the world!

Give What You Have

Neither the security nor the happiness of our Lord was tied to physical things. He could have possessed anything he desired, but his contentment had absolutely nothing to do with the physical. He was unimpressed with and unencumbered by *things*. Therefore, he never let his showing of hospitality be hindered by what he had or didn't have materially. We learn from him that hospitality has everything to do with meeting the needs of people, and little to do with the amount or the quality of the setting where it is practiced. His focus was on fellowship and love.

Did Jesus think it was wrong to have houses and possessions? We can know that the answer to that question is "No" as we see him reclining at the house of his friends in Bethany. God had blessed them with worldly wealth, and they were faithful stewards of what they had been given. They used their blessings to serve others. The point that Jesus made with his simple life was that contentment does not come because of anything we have or do not have.

The apostle Paul later modeled his contentment after Jesus, although he informs us it was something he *learned*:

> *I am not saying this because I am in need, for I have learned to be content whatever the circumstances. I know what it is to be in need, and I know what it is to have plenty. I have learned the*

15

secret of being content in any and every situation, whether well fed or hungry, whether living in plenty or in want. I can do everything through him who gives me strength (Philippians 4:11-13).

Further, he challenges us to follow his example of contentment by trusting that "God will meet all your needs according to his glorious riches in Christ Jesus" (Philippians 4:19). When we allow God to meet our spiritual and emotional needs, we can have a proper perspective on our physical needs.

Contentment is a prerequisite of effective hospitality. We often see our physical circumstances as vital to the practice of hospitality and let discontentment with these things hinder us from being hospitable. Nothing could be less like Jesus and his early leaders. They were concerned with loving people, not impressing them. Our clear call is to do the same, with or without nice possessions or living quarters. Contentment with our lives means being content with our marriages, children, salary, geographic location, and especially with the houses or apartments God has provided! Let's give up our love of the world (see 1 John 2:15), be content with our physical settings, and share what we have with open and humble hearts as Jesus did.

A Challenge to My Character!

Through the years, moving has provided the biggest challenge to my contentment level. Since Gordon and I married more than thirty years ago, we have lived in twenty-three different houses or apartments. As we have gotten older, our moving from one residence to another has not slowed down. Since moving to Boston seven years ago, we have lived in seven different places. Obviously, God has been working on my character to bring me to a deep understanding of contentment!

At our wedding, a soloist sang a song based on the book of Ruth containing these words: "Whither thou goest, I will go; whither thou lodgest, I will lodge." After having "lodged" in one house for my eighteen single years, I could not have imagined what the words of that song would mean in my married life! Had I been able to foresee the future at that time from my humble Louisiana roots, I would have fainted!

As a non-Christian, possessions were very important in my search for the great American Dream. By my mid-20s, Gordon and I had been successful in our pursuit of possessions. We had bought a house, sold it and bought a bigger one, acquired new furniture, cars, a fishing camp with lake frontage and a private pier, five acres of land on which to build our dream house, and numerous other items. During these early years, we saw each move as a step up the ladder of success. Although possessions seemed to provide security and contentment, the good feelings were short-lived. Soon the new wore off, and the feeling of emptiness returned.

The empty feelings were no doubt a big part of our motivation to seek lasting fulfillment in spiritual things. In our late 20s, we caught the dream of serving God full-time. We sold nearly all of our possessions and moved to another state for Gordon to attend a ministry training school. Our nice suburban home was exchanged for a dumpy apartment in a dangerous area, but we were happier and more content than we had ever been. It became clear just how little physical possessions figured in true happiness.

I was six months pregnant with our second child when Gordon completed his two years of training. We then moved two thousand miles from our parents and other close family. To add to the challenge, my favorite aunt (who was more like my grandmother) was dying of cancer. Now feelings of guilt and grief added to my burdens and made for a rough transition. In all of this, God was calling for me to be content. However, I had not yet learned the lesson. Instead, I learned to "stuff" my feelings and act content, while deep inside, I felt sorry for myself and for my children. God had much more work to do on my character!

In our numerous ministry moves, my focus was on the struggles of Gordon and the children and on helping them to be content. Although I poured myself into my work as a minister's wife and mother of two, contentment remained an elusive goal. My character did not ultimately change until I became a true disciple just before moving to Boston. I had been religious, but I did not have the indwelling power of the Holy Spirit to change my heart. I finally learned to put Philippians 4 into practice in dealing with my emotions. Praise God for these victories and for the deep sense of contentment present in my life now on a daily basis!

Contentment in Action

When we are not content, the showing of hospitality is forced and unnatural. However, when we are content, hospitality is a natural response to our gratitude. We want to share when we have something *to* share. We get excited about spreading love through hospitality, and our creative juices begin to flow. Crimped budgets and cramped living quarters will matter little when our hearts are full of love, joy and peace.

CONTENT,
BUT
NOT
COMPLACENT

As we talk of being content in all circumstances, we must be careful not to confuse contentment with complacency. We must not reason, "My surroundings don't matter. I must be content with these dark curtains that make my house seem depressing to everyone who enters." We can be resourceful and use what we have to brighten our homes, to make them welcoming no matter how humble. But we must not find our security in the amount of or the quality of the things we own.

Once we begin to imitate Jesus in meeting the needs of as many as possible, our relationships will blossom, and we will have joyous memories of serving others. Some of my best memories are when others lived with us during times of special need in their lives. We denied ourselves more than normal, sometimes giving up our bedroom for months at a time. The inconveniences proved to be minor, but the rewards were great. We can never out-give God; giving through hospitality is one of the best ways to discover this truth. Let's decide to be truly content and show hospitality like never before. It is a demonstration of the heart of God!

CHAPTER 2

Ordered, but Not Obsessive

HELEN WOOTEN

After each step of the creation process, "God saw that it was good" (Genesis). As he created order from the formless and empty earth, he was pleased. Throughout the first chapter of Genesis we can see God's plan emerge. We see how he put things together, making each part work beautifully with all the other parts.

As we create the foundation of our homes, we start with a house and then put into that house the order that reflects the nature of God; the same kind of order we see in the petals of flowers, in the feathers of birds, and in the consistency of the sunrise. The challenge for us is to reflect that same penchant for detail and order in our houses.

Another great example of God's order can be found in his instructions to the children of Israel as they were wandering in the wilderness. Exodus 25-27 records his plan for the building of the tabernacle. Every aspect of the building was exact and precise. No facet of this great undertaking was overlooked or considered unimportant. Then in Numbers 2 God gives specific instructions about the arrangement of the different tribes as they camped together. In Numbers 4 he gives instructions to the different clans of the Levites for moving the tabernacle from place to place. Each person had his particular task. Every time the Israelites pulled up camp, each Levite knew exactly what his responsibility was, exactly what he needed to carry to the new location. They weren't grabbing curtains and altars and scrambling to take the tent down. Even to the detail of carrying the tent pegs, they had their specific assignments.

Let's also look at God's ordered plan for the coming of Jesus. He began way back in Abraham's day (around 2000 B.C.), giving him the promise that he would bless the whole world through his seed. Then through the prophets Isaiah, Daniel, Joel and others, he predicted specifics about the coming of the Messiah. God kept following his plan through the birth and life of Jesus, and all the prophecies culminated at the resurrection. Because it is God's nature to stay with his plan, we thankfully now have salvation.

Order in Our Homes

As we look at these examples of order from the Scriptures, we see that if we are to have order in our lives and in our houses, we must also have a plan. Even though many of us today work outside our homes, proper planning can enable us to accomplish efficiently whatever needs to be done at home. Just as every office has its ordered way to get things done, so should every home.

Of course, even with the best efforts things do not always go according to our plans. Children get sick; parents get sick; or something comes up that needs immediate attention. All these things can distract us, but if we have a plan, we have something to return to, which will get us back on track.

For the most part, setting up specific things to do on specific days seems to be the best way to get started. This way we commit ourselves to accomplishing at least one or two tasks each day. For example, on Monday there always seems to be a lot of laundry after the weekend; so the laundry can be washed, folded and ironed, if needed, and clothes put away. The house usually needs a rather major cleaning each week, especially if there are children, so that could be the focus on another day. Grocery shopping could be accomplished on yet another day. For some people, making a daily list of things to be accomplished is a help. Beware: Too long a list can be overwhelming, and too short a list can be limiting.

Of course with any plan there needs to be flexibility, but not so much flexibility that work is not accomplished or that we make excuses about the lack of order in our homes. On the other hand, if we are too rigid, we can easily sin against our friends and family or anyone else who "interferes" with our routine. It is very important to have a joyful balance and to make sure that lack of order is not the norm. If we err in either direction, maintaining our homes becomes a burden, and we become grumblers and complainers, unable to rejoice in our responsibilities.

My Personal Plan Through the Years

While we were raising our five children, I soon realized that I needed to take every opportunity to get the work done—when the children were outside playing, when they were napping, or any five or ten minutes between activities. Life with small children can be a challenge but, like everything else, it can also be a victory; and having a plan is what can save the week.

When our first four were little, keeping the house neat and orderly was a challenge. Each evening after they were all in bed, I picked up anything out of place, cleaned the bathroom (after all those bedtime baths!), and only then would I sit down. Had I been a disciple, planning would have been even more crucial, as it is for disciples with families today. With very busy ministry schedules, our houses could look like children's playrooms much of the time if we are not consistent.

Taking time to think through my meals for the week helped me to write out a very specific grocery-shopping list. Therefore, I usually only went to the grocery store (with all my children) once a week. This helped not only in stress management, but in budget management as well.

I also needed a plan to keep the kitchen clean. I washed dishes as soon as dinner was over. When I got a dishwasher, I rinsed dishes and immediately put them into the dishwasher, washing the pots and pans and putting everything away in the cabinets. Now this is sometimes hard to do because of a group or one-on-one Bible study scheduled right after dinner. But the good thing about having a plan is that I can return to it before going to bed. That way I can start the day with a clean kitchen.

In order to take care of the mountains of dirty clothes that small children can create, my plan was to wash every day, but to iron only one day per week. Since we do not have children at home now with immediate clothing needs, doing the ironing once a week is more of a challenge and takes more discipline. There are just the two of us, so I could be more flexible than I ought to be and stretch the time between ironings (and not have clothes ready when we need them). I find that having my weekly plan and sticking to it helps me to maintain an ordered life just as much now as it did when my children were small. It is my conviction that this principle is true for singles' households as well. When everyone agrees upon a specific schedule for home management, everything runs more smoothly (even relationships!).

To take advantage of every opportunity, we must have two definite aspects of character: (1) a trained eye to see the chaos and (2) a mind-set that wants order in the home. Since I was trained by my mother in both of these areas, the only really difficult part for me was to do it and not to be lazy and indifferent. Becoming pregnant within the first year of our marriage, I discovered how quickly I could become self-indulgent and lazy. Morning sickness became my excuse not to get up. The excuse extended into the evening mealtime, so no dinner was prepared. For a while the sickness was legitimate, but as I look back, I know I should have held myself to some degree of order and productivity.

When I was growing up, my parents held me accountable; they taught and expected me to push through until the work was done...then I could rest. Isn't that God's way? He worked six days and rested on the seventh. Fortunately, as disciples, we have people in our lives to correct us if we are becoming lazy and to encourage us to push through and get our work done. It is then that rest is truly rewarding.

Be Open to Discipling

As disciples, even after learning how ordered God is and how we are to reflect his nature to others, we can rebel and be indifferent in the way we manage our homes. We may even have people in our lives giving us input and advice, but we consider it unimportant or intrusive. Some of us can think that those who disciple us are being too picky about unimportant details. But if this is the case, we need to go back and read Exodus 25-27 and Numbers 2 and 4 to see just how detailed God was in his instructions to the Israelites. And if we just do not seem to be able to get it together, we should keep asking for help. God will bless a heart that is willing and open and wants to learn.

Order is important to God; therefore, it must be important to us. There are many ways to get the work done, and it is up to us to find the best way, always being mindful that everything we do in our lives is to bring glory to God and to his kingdom.

CHAPTER 3

Consistent, but Not Compulsive

GERI LAING

God is "the same yesterday and today and forever" (Hebrews 13:8). Everything God is and does demonstrates his constancy and consistency—the flow of the seasons year after year, the coming of each new day, the utter reliability of his promises. God is always there, always working for our good, always working to sustain and maintain this world in which we live.

We are all greatly affected by our environment. Too many dark and dreary days can depress even the most positive and cheerful among us. On the other hand, a bright, clear spring day lightens our steps and lifts our spirits! The same is true of the places we live. How do you feel when you arrive home only to be greeted by dirty dishes all over the counter and in the sink, piles of dirty laundry in every room, unmade beds and filthy bathrooms? I don't know about you, but just the thought of this scene makes me feel burdened and depressed. We do not have to live like this, and in fact, disciples *must* not live like this! The real challenge, however, is not the great, inevitable cleanup; it is to keep it clean.

A Change of Mind and Heart

In my early years I certainly did not do much to imitate God in my personal surroundings. My unfortunate college roommate put up with a total slob, and even my husband, during our first years of marriage, must have been quite frustrated by my lack of order and neatness. Even an "eye for color" and some ability to decorate didn't do much good when it was surrounded by chaos! Of course, even in my most undisciplined, messy years, I did occasionally "clean up" and "clean out." But the order was short-lived because I didn't consistently live with order and discipline in my life!

As the years have gone by, however, I have become more convicted of God's desire for order and discipline. As God's child, everything in my life is a reflection of God himself. What a privilege and what an incredible challenge! My home is my little bit of creation, and the way I keep it speaks volumes about my view of God, of myself, and of my family and guests.

Most of us are able to at least straighten up our homes, apartments or rooms. Perhaps we do it under the duress of expected company, or maybe we have just reached the point of, "I can't stand this mess any longer!" The frustration comes because, once we have everything cleaned up, we cannot seem to keep it that way. The great challenge is to keep a home that is clean and neat while still allowing those who live there the freedom to do just that—*live!* We are a people of extremes: We either don't care enough about creating homes that are neat, clean and attractive, or we are obsessed with the state of our surroundings, becoming selfish, greedy and unloving. God made a beautiful world and he keeps it that way. Why? So we can live in it and enjoy it. So should be the state of our personal surroundings, our homes!

I asked my children how they felt about having a clean house. They talked about how important it was for them to be able to bring their friends to a neat and attractive home. We tend to think children don't care about these things, but in fact, they do. Their friends have often commented that our home seemed so nice and "cleaned up." My children also went on to describe how they felt when they visited other people's homes that were messy or dirty. They all expressed embarrassment for their friends and their friends' families.

Once we are convinced that cleanliness and order should be maintained on a consistent, daily basis, what are some of the practical things we can do to bring this about?

Every Day

Make your bed first thing in the morning! It's amazing how much nicer a bedroom can look by just making the bed. It only takes a few minutes, but it is one of those things that is hard to get back to once the day begins.

When the children were young, I usually put only a fitted bottom sheet on their beds. Since each had a blanket they used at night, they only had to fold it and pull up a bedspread to make their beds. This was a part of their morning routine.

Keep the kitchen cleaned up and uncluttered. Get into the habit of cleaning up after every meal. Keep dishes washed and put away or rinsed and in a dishwasher whenever they are used, and teach your entire family to do the same. Teach everyone to clean "as they go," keeping crumbs and spills wiped and swept up. Does the microwave need cleaning or the stove top wiping? Do these things when you notice them; it takes about thirty seconds when we do them as we go.

I keep only a few decorative things on my kitchen counters. Everything else has its own place. Have you ever really looked at the small appliances that are probably covering your counter space? Most of them are certainly not very attractive, they are quite bulky, and we really do not use them as often as we might think. The only appliance I leave out is my coffeemaker. Everything else I store in convenient, out-of-sight places: under counters or in drawers. This goes a long way toward making a kitchen look clean and in order.

Straighten up before you go to bed. Pick up the little odds and ends still lying around at the end of the day: children's toys, cast-off shoes and unhung jackets. There is nothing worse than greeting a fresh new day with clutter and confusion. It makes me feel burdened and overwhelmed before the day has really even begun!

Don't forget the dirty clothes. For those with small families, laundry may not be a tremendous burden and can be done once or twice a week. However, for those with larger families the laundry can be one of the most overwhelming tasks of the week. As soon as everything is finally washed, dried, folded and put away, several more loads appear out of nowhere! These suggestions may help:

Teach everyone to bring their dirty clothes, sheets or towels to a laundry room or designated place at the end of the day.

Start a load of wash first thing in the morning and sort out the next load.

Folding clothes is a great job for older children, especially when they are sitting and watching television. Teach them to fold and put the clean clothes and laundry in the appropriate rooms.

Every Week

Get rid of the dust and dirt. Most houses need a good dusting once a week and a thorough vacuuming once or twice a week. Keep up with it and it's a breeze; let it go and it's miserable.

Clean those bathrooms! Bathrooms that are cleaned well once a week tend to stay clean and don't take nearly the time to clean as those that are only dealt with when the slime of mildew and the scum of neglect have begun to grow.

Again, teach everyone to clean and wipe up as they go: dirty clothes should be taken to the laundry basket, towels hung, toothbrushes and toothpaste put away, floors swept. As in the kitchen, organize so that very little is left out on the counters and everything has a specific storage place.

If you need help, get it. Maintaining a home is a challenge to the most disciplined among us! Keeping a clean home seems next to impossible for mothers who juggle both families and jobs. Professional help every week or two for those who can afford it can take a tremendous pressure off a busy family. And even though a professional cleaning service is not in many of our budgets, there is still a way to get help. I have often hired an older high school student or a college student to clean for two or three hours each week. It takes a load off me to have my bathrooms thoroughly cleaned and my house dusted. If she has time, she may run the vacuum cleaner. When those things are done, I can keep up with the rest fairly comfortably. I pay her more than she can make babysitting or even at a minimum-wage job, so it's worth it for her, and yet I still pay less than I would pay a cleaning service.

Every So Often

Get rid of the things you don't need and use. Several years ago when we moved to North Carolina, we had to store most of our belongings while we lived temporarily in a small apartment. "Temporary" turned out to be nearly a year. Some of the stored things we really needed and missed, but I was truly amazed at how many things we never missed at all. When we finally did move into our home, I didn't want to crowd it with all the "things" we didn't need. We had several garage sales, sold items in the newspaper, gave things away, and finally just threw away large amounts of clutter. My rule of thumb is: If you haven't used it, worn it, or looked at it for close to a year, toss it. You'll never miss it! It is uncanny; we can regularly pare down our possessions, but they always seem to "grow back." Several times a year, I go through closets and cabinets searching for what is outgrown, never used, worn-out or broken. My children and husband have sometimes thought me to be a bit heartless as I threw away rubber-band balls, torn-up t-shirts, two-year-old schoolwork, paper-clip chains, fossilized Halloween candy and various other sentimental items, but even God declares that there is "a time to keep and a time to throw away" (Ecclesiastes 3:6)!

Everyone Helps

As I have often told my children, "We all live here, we all make the mess, so we all clean it up." It is amazing how much easier it is to maintain a home when everyone helps. Children can do much more than we often expect of them, and it is important for them to learn to be responsible and to do things well. From a young age children can be taught where toys belong and can be expected to put them there. Older children can do many things, from keeping their own rooms clean and straightened, to doing the dishes and cleaning up the kitchen, folding clothes, dusting and vacuuming. (Just remember that they are not slaves or indentured servants, but rather, loved and cherished members of a family!)

Put these things into practice and watch as chaos begins to subside, laughter is restored, and even your blood pressure returns to normal. As you begin to enjoy the results of these changes, however, be careful that the pendulum does not swing too far in the *other* direction! Just as I once was irresponsible and undisciplined, which was reflected in my surroundings, I now struggle with a different problem: I sometimes care *too* much about our home's appearance. God's world reflects his heart of love, and my home also expresses my heart. I therefore want it to be a testament of my love and care for people, rather than a mirror of frustration and impatience. Unfortunately, developing this balance is much easier said than done.

There are a few things that I have had to accept and continually remember about the work of running a home and a household:

1. It will *never* be *all* done.
2. It will *never* be perfect.
3. It will *never* stay that way.

Accept these facts, and it will be so much easier to relax and enjoy life.

Our homes are for living, and living is for people. We must not ever forget that. One day our children will be grown and gone. Yes, they will remember and appreciate all the ways we physically took care of them and met their needs (probably more than they do now). But above all, they will remember and cherish the things we did together in our homes: the laughter, the hugs, the jokes, the good times. They will remember the family times more than the family room, the bedtime talks and stories more than the bedroom, and the mealtimes together more than the meals themselves. The same is true of all those who will have come through our homes. The love and joy they experienced there will be remembered long after the messes are cleaned up and order is restored. If I could add a verse on to 1 Corinthians 13, God's chapter on love, it would be: "If I am able to clean my house until it shines and polish it

CONSISTENT,
BUT
NOT
COMPULSIVE

until it sparkles, but have not love, it is no more than an empty shell and is worth nothing!"

Let us, therefore, imitate our awesome Creator and loving Father by reflecting in our own tiny pieces of creation the love, compassion and beauty he has lavished upon us.

CHAPTER 4

Creative, but Not Consumed

JEANIE SHAW

In the beginning God created the heavens and the earth. Now the earth was formless and empty, darkness was over the surface of the deep, and the spirit of God was hovering over the waters. And God said, "Let there be..." (Genesis 1:1-3).

From absolutely nothing, the incredible wonders of nature came to be...God, our Father, the Master, making something from nothing. We admire an inspiring theater presentation, a colorful display of fireworks, a classic work of art and a highly trained orchestra. We might "ooh" and "aah" and even give it a standing ovation. Yet, however magnificent, these things pale in comparison to the majesty of the Master Creator.

Walk for a moment through God's showcase of the heavens and the earth. On a dark night, look at the formations of the countless stars, and imagine being there when the stars first sang. Watch until you see one dart through the atmosphere. As it goes through its faithful phases, see the moon cast a diamond-like sparkle across the water. In the daylight, watch the clouds roll by and the birds in pattern, migrating south.

Attend God's light shows. A sunrise over the mountains or a sunset across a bay. Hear the thunder crackle with explosive power as the sky lights up. Notice the sculpting of God's hands with the terra-cotta mountains of the Southwest to the snow-capped peaks of the Far East. Listen, and be calmed by the sounds of the ocean's roar, the birds' singing and the fire's crackling.

Let the colors of the autumn leaves, the feathers of the peacock and the petals of the orchid inspire you.

Be reminded of the smells of cut grass, a flower garden in full bloom, the spray of the ocean or food roasting over an open fire.

Try to imagine the fun God had as he created puppies and watched them play, as he stretched the neck of the giraffe and striped the zebra, as he made caterpillars fuzzy and positioned the legs of the praying mantis.

Be impressed, be amazed with our Creator and read on.

The Author of Creativity

> *Then God said, "Let us make man*
> *in our image, in our likeness."*
> *...So God created man in his own image,*
> *in the image of God he created him;*
> *male and female he created them (Genesis 1:26-27).*

We were fashioned by God. Intricately formed and knit together. Created in his image. The very first thing we learn about God in the Bible is that he created. God, the Author of creation, is creative. Since we are created by him in his image, we are made to be creative.

I am convinced that many believe they are not creative people. We are blessed with different gifts and differing degrees of talent, but we are all created in God's image. Therefore, we are all creative. To believe we are not creative is to deny who God is. We must get a conviction about this and awaken the sleepy creativity within ourselves. It takes effort. We cannot be lazy in our minds and be creative at the same time. Being creative in our homes and our lives takes time and effort. Imagine if God had not taken such time and effort in creation. The world might be black and white, with no sound and only the smell of burning chemicals. What if he had not taken care to order the sunrise and sunset or the human anatomy? The thought and energy made it spectacular—a gift for us, his creation, to enjoy. We are born with an innate desire to reflect our Creator. Yet, sin and the challenges of life can harden us to that spiritual quality if we let them.

On a recent visit to a third-world country, I was impressed with the people who make their homes upon trash heaps. As I walked through their community, I realized that they express themselves individually in the way they order and decorate their very humble abodes. Creativity comes to life in a place that could engulf its inhabitants with gloom and depression. God created (designed and decorated) the home he made for us, his creation. The heavens and the earth reflect him as the humble huts I saw reflect their owners. His handiworks let us know something about him, and inspire us to be more like him:

> *The heavens declare the glory of God;*
> *the skies proclaim the work of his hands.*
> *Day after day they pour forth speech;*
> *night after night they display knowledge.*

There is no speech or language
where their voice is not heard.
Their voice goes out into all the earth,
their words to the ends of the world (Psalm 19:1-4).

For since the creation of the world God's invisible qualities—
his eternal power and divine nature—have been clearly seen,
being understood from what has been made, so that men are
without excuse (Romans 1:20).

Reflecting God's Glory

Does your home reflect the glory of God? Of God in you? Does the creative energy you put into it with color, design, sound, light, plants and fun cause those who enter to feel warm, happy, peaceful and "at home"? Or does your home more resemble "before creation"—formless and empty, plain and boring? Does it represent the chaos of mankind, clothing strewn about, junky and cluttered?

In six days God created everything, and then he rested. Can you imagine if each week God recreated the animals, flowers, etc.? "No more chicken this week. You will now eat roasted gazoo and have purple gazoo eggs for breakfast." Life would be consumed with just keeping up with all the changes. The circle of life would become zigzagged!

In six days creation was completed. It was very good, and on the seventh day God rested. There is a lesson in this. Put your awakened creative energy to work. If you believe your creativity is still sluggish, pull in someone whose creativity is so high it will spark yours. Ask him or her to help you set a realistic goal for your house to be a reflection of God's presence in your life—even if the transformation is as gradual as one room a month. But never get so *preoccupied* with decorating that you forget to *be occupied* with having people in your home. Decorating your home is not your purpose; showing God's love to others is.

You may need to first get rid of cluttering "junk" in your house. Garage sales are wonderful, and seldom, if ever, will you miss some item you sold in one.

Get ideas from others about decorating your house. Take note of styles you see and like in others' homes, and then imitate them.

Pay attention to the kinds of things God decorates with. For example, bright lights make the house alive and cheery. Light-colored paint and mirrors add to the brightness. For a peaceful, more romantic feel, use dim lights and/or candlelight. Lighting that emphasizes some plants or a favorite picture or painting adds a lot.

Sounds also help set the mood in the house. The sound of the TV blaring is a sure way to take the focus off people, both household members and guests. It does not set a hospitable tone. I have a few favorite tapes and CDs that are great background music for conversation or dinner.

Use colors that complement each other and group pictures attractively. Pictures of children and by children, displayed attractively, are fun to have in the house and make the children feel special. Keep beds made and counters and tables free from clutter. Don't forget the bathrooms! Plants and pictures make a big difference here, too. Let the children's rooms reflect their personalities as they help to decorate them. (Train them to be creative.) Decorating for the holidays gives a hospitable charm and helps make family memories.

Making Something out of Nothing

Creativity is fun! It will help make your house feel like home to you and others. And it doesn't have to cost a lot of money. I'll give you some examples from our first—and very humble—home. I knew how I wanted it to look because of the way my sister had decorated her house and because of examples I'd seen in various places. When we first married, my husband and I owned one broken chair and had an income that classified with the government as poverty level. We started our family soon after, and realized that new furniture was a luxury we definitely could not afford. Ingenuity was the need of the hour. We found our sofa by the roadside. Someone was redecorating and had thrown it away. It needed recovering, so I did what I could and got help for the rest. I worked out an exchange of something I could give (like meals) for someone else's expertise and help. An unwanted bed became ours. We stained an empty electric-wire spool, decorated it with rope around the edges and transformed it into our kitchen table. Grandmother's old chairs, stripped and stained, became our kitchen chairs. Then while riding through our neighborhood, I saw someone replacing their carpet. They didn't like the color; I did. Their old carpet became our new carpet. An empty room needed a sitting area. With a hammer, nails, some wood, fabric and a sewing machine to make cushions, it was done. For the baby's room came another roadside find—an old chest that came alive with bright paint and wallpaper cutouts.

For our walls, baskets were cheap...so they became the decor. A few added ribbons gave them a "homey touch." We framed and hung pictures from calendars and an embroidery project, which I had never done before (and will never do again!). A little fabric from sheets and remnants, someone who knew what they were doing, and a sewing machine turned the plain windows into dressed windows. Plants made it come alive as they can "cover a multitude of sins." One week and $100 later, it was done! I looked at it, saw that it was good, and rested.

Our God is an awesome Master Creator. Let us do him honor, reflecting his creativity, glory and majesty in every aspect of our lives and in every room of our homes.

Part II

·HOME·

Finally, all of you,
live in harmony with one another;
be sympathetic, love as brothers,
be compassionate and humble.

1 PETER 3:8

CHAPTER 5

God's Plan for Home

SHEILA JONES

Whether cave, hut or castle, human beings have always sought the security of home. Shelter from wind and rain and snow. A place uniquely ours where we can gather our family around us and feel the warmth of their closeness. Home is much more than "house." It has to do with what fills the house, with nesting and nurturing. It speaks of belonging.

In the Bible the word "home" is used 195 times. Over and over again the concordance reads, "he went home" or "they returned home." At the end of a battle, it was a joy to go home. When you were hurting, it was comforting to go home. If you were a captive, it was exhilarating finally to go home. Ask any POW in a camp, "What would it mean to you to go home?" You would not see any hesitation in answering your question. You would see a longing eye, a quivering lip. Home is safety. Home is privacy. Home truly is where the heart is.

But such a blessing can be used to satisfy our own selfish desires. Some want to be home so they can do what they want to do—sometimes that *doing* is sinful, and even destructive, to others. People construct bombs in the privacy of their homes. They rape and kill. They watch pornographic movies. They read trashy novels. They beat their spouses and abuse their children. Just because we are in our own house, does not mean we are building "home."

To create home as God intended is to show love and respect for each member of the family. It is to think of the needs of others and not just of our own needs. The world beats us down, whether at work or school or play. We need to know that we can come home and be loved and accepted even if we have big noses or acne or bad haircuts. At home, they will laugh with us, but not at us (at least not for long).

Alzheimer's patients often say, "I want to go home." I read of one case in which a family took their father to every house he had lived in to see if one of them registered as "home." He responded to none of the houses. To him, home was more a state of familiar comfortableness than it was a place. Because his mind was not in its normal state, he felt displaced and not at home in any physical setting.

Growing Up

I am eternally grateful to my own parents for teaching me the definition of "home." My parents were not perfect, but they were gentle lovers of God. They consistently encouraged our interests and believed in us. Never did I question whether my parents loved me. When I opened the door to our home, I always knew I was safe in every sense of the word. Unlike some of my friends, I never feared what might be happening at home if I brought someone with me. Because of that environment, I grew up thinking that everyone liked me, and as a result, I generally approached new people and new situations with confidence.

When I brought friends home with me, Mom always had a warm hug for all of us. She was the type who made each person feel that he or she was the most special to her. She lived life with a childlike enthusiasm—the wonder of nature, the warmth of friendship, the certainty of faith. Pretension found no place in her character. She was much more aware of others than she was of herself; whether it was an awkward preteen, a disenfranchised single mom, a backward middle-aged woman; all were special to my mom. She gave little or no consideration as to how someone could better her social status. She was a giver. She was a gift.

My father was a soft-spoken man who, along with my mother, loved to laugh. He loved to see us enjoy life with our friends. He would massage my feet late at night and talk to me about his growing-up years. He seldom raised his voice at us; he was firm but flexible.

My mother died about ten years ago, and since my father had Alzheimer's disease, we had to sell the family home. We had moved there when I was four years old. When I first saw the "For Sale" sign in the front yard, I stood there and sobbed. A passerby stopped to ask if I was okay, and I explained through my tears, "I will be; it's just that my mom died and we are selling the house that has always been home to me." Memories flooded my mind...times we had spent together in that white stucco house. It hurt to think that I could never again go "home." But in the hurt, I was thankful that I had been privileged to know what home was and that I could give to my children and others what my parents had given to me.

Building My Own Home

I am aware that not all people have the example of their own homelife upon which to build "home." But had I not had that example, I could have learned from other disciples, and I could have learned from the

Scriptures about families and relationships in general. I could have learned to be gentle with my children (Proverbs 15:1; Ephesians 6:4), to welcome strangers and friends alike (Romans 12:13), to laugh and to enjoy life (Proverbs 15:13, 31:25; 1 Peter 3:10), to encourage the interests of others and to feel their pain (Philippians 2:4; Romans 12:15), and to provide a safe environment for my family and friends (1 Peter 3:8-9).

I am personally grateful that I did not have to work outside the home when our three girls were younger. I am thankful to have welcomed them in from school (except those few times I returned home late to find them sitting on the front porch in dismay). I look back and love hearing the door slam as they came and went (at that point in time, however, there was nothing sweet about that sound). I kissed their boo-boos and disciplined them for their own good (they did not believe that then, but they do now).

In our current culture, more women than ever must work to support or to help support the family. I am convinced that if our hearts are committed to God, he will help us as mothers and/or fathers to create "home" even if we cannot physically be with our children as much as we would like. But this can only happen if we have our priorities straight and are not seeking our sense of worth and self-esteem from our jobs.

Keeping a Proper Perspective

Ultimately, a sense of home starts in the heart of the one building it. Home can be in a tent on the campground. It can be in a motel room for several weeks in the midst of a job transfer. Home can even be in someone else's house as they share it with us.

As disciples, though, we must be careful not to become so sentimental about building home that we would not go anywhere or do anything for the sake of the gospel. Our children attended five different schools within a five-year period. Psychologists would raise an eyebrow at such upheaval in their development. We certainly know it was difficult on them, especially our oldest who was in middle school and high school at the time. But since each move was made out of a prayerful consideration of the spiritual needs of our family and of the church, we trusted that God would take care of our children. I am thankful to say that he has done just that. We have now been in the Boston area for eight years, and each of our girls (16, 19 and 23 years) is a committed disciple who thanks us regularly for making faithful decisions during her formative years.

The bottom line is: To build home, we must first lay a foundation of obedience to God who is, himself, the masterbuilder of home. In speaking of God's family, the church, Peter gives us a description of home as God intends:

> *Finally, all of you, live in harmony with one another; be sympathetic, love as brothers, be compassionate and humble. Do not repay evil with evil or insult with insult, but with blessing, because to this you were called so that you may inherit a blessing (1 Peter 3:8-9).*

One of the blessings we will "inherit" is a homelife that will encourage our spouses, our children and everyone who enters our houses. It's no wonder heaven is described as being "at home with the Lord" (2 Corinthians 5:8).

CHAPTER 6

A Godly Atmosphere

SHELLEY METTEN

The moment we walk into a home, we receive some kind of impression. What we see, what we hear, what we smell puts the experience together and gives us a feeling about that home. The atmosphere of our homes is a reflection of our hearts for the people who come to share that home with us.

Having had the opportunity to be in homes all over the world, from the wealthiest to the poorest in the kingdom, I have found this proverb to be true:

> *By wisdom a house is built,*
> *and through understanding it is established;*
> *through knowledge its rooms are filled with rare*
> *and beautiful treasures (Proverbs 24:3-4).*

By Wisdom a House Is Built

According to this proverb, we build our homes through the wisdom that comes from God, and it comes with the highest standard of expectation for our lives. James' description of that wisdom gives us a good idea of the atmosphere that should permeate our homes:

> *But the wisdom that comes from heaven is first of all pure; then peace-loving, considerate, submissive, full of mercy and good fruit, impartial and sincere (James 3:17).*

We can read this passage and test ourselves and our roommates or families to see how we are doing in promoting a godly atmosphere that welcomes and encourages others to join us. Are we reflecting the nature of God and his wisdom? In this chapter we will look at two of the attributes mentioned by James: peace-loving and sincere. Perhaps in your own study times you can consider the other six.

Peace-Loving

Are the people in your home committed to creating a peaceful atmosphere? This requires overlooking the little hurts and loving beyond the moment to treasure unity and forgiveness in our families. There is never a time for destructive language, bitterness, slamming doors, cool silence, or even staying hidden in a room, unwilling to communicate.

Our children were never allowed to speak in an angry tone to each other. Obviously there would be times of disagreement, but they had to find a way to express what they felt without retaliation. Adults, likewise, have not been given special permission from God to be rude and insensitive.

A peace-loving home does not necessarily mean a quiet home, and the Metten family home is far from quiet. At the dinner table it is difficult to follow the flow of the conversation because everyone is excited to share his or her view. It is just so much fun to be together! There are certainly moments when the atmosphere becomes tense, but each one of us gets involved in bringing the situation to a positive conclusion. If the problem is between my daughter Jennifer and me, my husband Greg and son Matt both help us to have a godly response to each other by helping us to see our own faults. This kind of honest communication helps each of us to feel loved and secure.

Recently I received a phone call from a college student who had lived with us for a short time a few years ago. He made some bad choices and basically left the church and his relationship with God for a while. We loved him a lot, and it was a painful time for all of us, especially our kids. He had come back and was stronger than ever. When he called, one of the things he said was, "I would like to come to your home and have a meal with your family. I miss those times together." A peace-loving home definitely has a powerful attraction and impacts people.

Sincere

It will never work to put on the pretense of a warm, inviting home. An insincere heart is one of the easiest attitudes to discern; people feel uncomfortable around those who are fake. If we are sincere, people will feel it and be attracted to us. The people in our family will certainly know if we are being insincere because once the door is closed and the friends are gone, we will be different. If that is what happens in your home, then you are teaching that it is okay to say one thing and then do another. If you are self-controlled when others are around and yell at each other when by yourselves, you will destroy your family and your influence on others.

Being sincere means that you have the *heart* of a servant, not just the *skills* of a servant. It means that you want to help, not just that you are expected to help. Sincerity is an attitude of the heart, not just a lifestyle.

When we lived in India, our days were long, tiring and at times very emotionally challenging. But every evening before we all went to sleep, we would sit on the bed and play a few games of hearts and talk. It was a bonding time for our family and anyone else who might be there with us. We would talk and laugh and sometimes even cry together. The sincerity born in those special times together bonded us and caused our home to be warm and inviting to others who joined us from time to time.

Recently someone asked me what had been my favorite place to live. My response came easily...Bombay, India. Although we lived in other Indian cities, Bombay will always be dear to my heart as our first Indian home. There I learned what it means to be sincerely cared for. There was one Indian family in particular who brought me into their home and accepted me as part of their family, the family of a woman named Rosie Athaide. She would spend her last rupee to buy a bottled drink for me to protect my health. Whenever I was sad, it was to Rosie's house that I headed for encouragement and guidance. Six family members lived in one room in that home, but they always found a place for me.

Rooms Filled with Rare and Beautiful Treasures

Many Indian Christian homes are only one room, but in that one room can be found all of the treasures of God. You will rarely find expensive furniture and fine china, but from the moment you walk into the room, you will be served and loved. All of your needs will be met, and you will feel like a dignitary in a wealthy Indian palace. The rare and beautiful treasure of a home is the safe and loving atmosphere created there.

If we are to fill our rooms with the rare and beautiful treasure of a godly atmosphere, we must take time to plan. It will not just spontaneously happen. Chaos communicates a message to others to stay away. The secret to having an orderly home is to be organized. For years I have sat down one day a week and planned my menus for the entire week. I take time to think through each day and consider the needs of each family member and the special things I can do for them. I also consider friends that we need to include in a family meal and any special needs they might have. The week always includes a family night dinner and devotional with our family (and others we want to include). Whenever anyone walks into our home, there is food already prepared and an enthusiastic welcome.

A
GODLY
ATMOSPHERE

If we are disorganized and the week is running us, there is not much enthusiasm for unexpected visitors or individual needs in our home. Having a plan makes a busy home feel relaxed and inviting. People don't see the planning, but they feel the effects of it.

How would your home be described if someone walked in unannounced today? Would the treasure that fills each room be an atmosphere that is inviting and warm? Would there be a sense of protection and concern for each person, family or guest?

We must build our homes with wisdom and create the rare and beautiful treasure of a godly atmosphere—the same atmosphere Jesus is preparing for us:

> "In my Father's house are many rooms...I am going there to prepare a place for you. And if I go and prepare a place for you, I will come back and take you to be with me that you also may be where I am" (John 14:2-3).

CHAPTER 7

Building and Sharing Family

GLORIA BAIRD

"Home is where the heart is." Building family begins in the heart. Family hits at our emotions, our deep roots. As I thought about building family, I first tried to recall how Al and I built our family. But soon my thoughts went back to my own childhood and experience of family as I grew up. I was surprised at the flow of tears that came as I remembered our home and family—Mother and Daddy, my older brother, David, and later my grandfather and cousin, Billy, who came to live with us when my grandmother died. My tears were mixed with thankfulness and sadness—thankfulness for the rich heritage of love I have been given; sadness because I lost my mother this past January, and with her death came a sense of losing "home."

As long as I can remember, family also meant lots of uncles, aunts and cousins plus a continual flow of people of different nationalities who came either to visit or to live with us. We did not live in plush surroundings, but when people came to our home, they were genuinely loved and welcomed with warm hugs and homemade chocolate chip cookies from my mom's well-known cookie jar. After Mother's death, one of my most prized keepsakes was that cookie jar. Though of very little monetary value, it is a cherished symbol to me of our family life.

To some, remembering family can bring tears because of hurts, pain, neglect and abuse. Today's family must be described with added words such as "traditional," "nuclear," "dysfunctional," "single-parent," "composite," "blended," etc. We will be like our parents in both good and bad ways. Often family traits, habits and traditions are carried on without even realizing it because discipling is a universal principle that works. Fortunately, when we are born into God's family, God gives us a new heart and reshapes our view of family according to the truth of his Word. Our part in this reshaping is being open and eager for training and continual input.

Closeness in Immediate Family

As Al and I began our marriage, we consciously imitated aspects of my parents' relationship that we admired: praying together, having daily devotionals, saying "I love you," showing affection (kissing "hello" and "good-bye" and after mealtime prayers). Those early marriage habits set the tone for a solid spiritual and emotional base for Al and me and our three daughters. From their earliest years we taught and expected our girls to be close to God, to us as their parents, and to each other.

Close to God

For our children's hearts to be totally devoted to God we must pray for them before they are born and continue to pray for them and with them afterwards. In Deuteronomy 6 God's command to teach and train our children as we go about our daily routine is the key to a spiritual family. Some of our best talks about God and his love and care were in the car as I drove the girls from place to place, and at night as they were getting ready for bed. Their deepest thoughts and biggest concerns seemed to come out more easily at those relaxed times.

Dinner time proved to be the best time for us to pull our family together. It was a time to turn off TV, ignore the phone, share special events or problems of the day, and focus on God and lessons from his Word. Weekly family devotionals were great training times for the girls to pray aloud, lead favorite songs and to plan and present lessons. We memorized Bible verses that we remember to this day, and we frequently played Bible games. These times were vital to show how to implement God's principles practically in their daily experiences.

Close to Parents

The most significant factors that pulled our family close, next to our love for God, were our love for each other as husband and wife and our unity as we trained our girls. Never underestimate the power of outward expressions of love and affection between parents. Although our girls acted embarrassed at our kissing after our mealtime prayers, now our married daughters and their husbands (and many other couples around the world) have made that a habit too. Most importantly, our loving each other as husband and wife second only to God, gave our girls security and trained them to love their husbands above their children.

In training and disciplining children, unity between parents is key. At one time or another all three of our girls tried the "divide and conquer" technique with "But Dad said I could..." or "Let's ask Mom. She'll let us...." When they saw our unified stance or were aware that we worked through any differences to a point of unity, they ultimately felt secure and loved, though maybe disappointed initially.

We learned all sorts of life lessons helping the girls with their physics and calculus, working in the kitchen together, planting and tending the garden, going to the emergency room for stitches, selling Girl Scout cookies, and tearfully burying our little dog, Buttons. It is vital to make the most of the time spent together and to be available and accessible. Parents need to be alert to the times and situations in which each child is the most open and eager to talk—then be available.

Close to Each Other As Siblings

Our family was close in more ways than one. We lived in a small three bedroom/one bathroom house during our girls' growing-up years. Interestingly, what we would consider a disadvantage today really was an advantage in training our girls to cooperate, share and repent of self-ishness. Al and I had an expectation for our girls that they love—*and like*—each other. I often reminded them that sisters can be friends. We treated them with respect and demanded respectful interactions first with us and then with each other. For instance, saying "Shut up!" to someone was not allowed. Our family nights were special memory-mak-ing times. We took turns choosing what meal we wanted, and the girls often worked together to prepare it. A favorite choice on a snowy night was cheese fondue served by the fireplace followed by a devotional and a game of Aggravation.

Extending Family to Others

One of the richest blessings of having strong family ties is bringing others in, whether short term or long, to share the love and warmth. In Matthew 25:34-40 Jesus makes it clear that when we care for others, we are caring for him. We had to open up our home by first opening up our hearts! We have seen God enrich our lives through every person who came into our home. Not every experience was a positive one, but even then we learned some very important lessons.

Doing the best with what you have is a vital principle in extending family to others. We could not refuse to invite people into our home because we did not have a spare bedroom or an extra bathroom. Typi-cally one of the girls' bedrooms was designated as a guest room and could quickly be rearranged for anyone coming to stay with us. The bathroom schedule certainly had to be planned out and communicated to everyone involved. We all remember a youth rally weekend when around twenty girls stayed with us, and yes, with one bathroom! I think they really felt family!

There is no better place for learning and growing than having people live with us. We all are seen and see each other in action daily. Just as we taught and trained our girls on a daily basis, so we have had opportunity to teach and train others in basics such as cooking, cleaning and budgeting. As we included them in our lives, they experienced family devotionals, fun times, our daily time with God and our interactions—"bumps" too—and we saw theirs as well.

We have had people of all ages and backgrounds stay with us: children whose parents couldn't care for them, several people with emotional instabilities, teens off the street, families with young children, families from other countries, singles without jobs, very stable and responsible singles, married couples with severe problems and strong, spiritual couples. All the different people who have been in our home are intertwined in our lives and hearts in a very special way. We have more "children" and "grandchildren" than we would ever have imagined!

What a responsibility and privilege we have as Christians to communicate God's sense of true family in today's world! Family makes a difference! Family gives us a belonging place! As we build family God's way, we will radiate love and support which will draw others to him—and to the church, his family.

CHAPTER 8

Singles' Household As Family

INGA OSTRANDER

It was Saturday night at 12:30—or should I say Sunday morning—when I arrived home for the first time since 7:30 A.M. My day had been incredibly busy and I was completely exhausted. I had coordinated a wedding and reception and was particularly happy about how well both had gone. During the drive home I began to think about how quickly my morning would come. I thought to myself, *I'll get up early, spend some great time in Bible study and prayer, go to the grocery store and begin preparing lunch.* I had invited a few other Christians and a friend who was studying the Bible to come over after church.

Looking forward to a short but great night's sleep, I walked into the home I shared with three other single women disciples only to find that disaster had struck. The living room was in disarray. Glasses and things had been left around and pillows tossed in an unusual manner. The state of the dining room brought more disappointment. The tablecloth was soiled, dirty dishes and glasses were scattered about. *Okay,* I thought to myself, *I'm disappointed, but this shouldn't take too much time to clean in the morning.*

At this point it was still looking hopeful for my Sunday lunch plans, but then I turned the corner and saw the kitchen. It looked like something out of a Garfield comic strip. My mouth fell open in astonishment. Food was hanging off dishes that were strewn across the kitchen table and every inch of counter and stovetop. Pots and pans had food adhering to the sides. Various unknown particles were on the floor; dessert dishes had what looked like Elmer's glue stuck to each one. I think you get the picture. My heart fell to my toes with a thud of discouragement. I had never seen our home like this. I wanted to believe I had taken a wrong turn on the highway and this really wasn't our house. Visions of spending endless hours cleaning raced through my mind when I finally decided to call it a night.

Morning came more quickly than I had hoped. Fortunately, God knew the anguish and desperation I felt to make the lunch after church a special time. Shortly after waking up, I heard my roommate, who had thrown the dinner party the night before, mutter before she headed out the door, "I'm really sorry about the mess; I'll clean it up after church."

Wanting to avoid conflict, I figured I would just take care of things myself. But, deciding I had to do what was right, I asked her to wait so that we could talk about how I was feeling about the state of the house and the plans I had for lunch. After a difficult discussion, my roommate realized what was right and stayed to clean up before she went to church. In establishing our household we had agreed upon certain principles that enabled us to work through this conflict.

Why Build Family?

Some singles might, and do, ask, "Why should I work to build family? I've left my parents' home, and I haven't gotten married yet. I am a free-to-do-my-own-thing single. Trying to do things with others in my household is too hard to coordinate." The main thing single disciples need to remember is that they are just that: disciples. As disciples of Jesus we are called to love our brothers and sisters with heart and actions, to lay down our lives for them, to share our possessions with them, to confess our sins to them, to pray for and with them, to meet their needs, to build them up. Is this not even more required and needed in our everyday living situations? As disciples, we are born into God's family and become members of his household. What better place to experience and exemplify the family of God than in our own houses and apartments in relationships with those who live with us?

Some singles have a wrong view of being single. They want to wait until they are married to start developing their character to be more selfless and giving, more hospitable, more vulnerable, more available to listen and more concerned about the cleanliness of the home. I have a deep conviction that we are who we are right now. Our character doesn't suddenly change the day we say "I do." A lifestyle that is independent and resistant to building family is not at all like that of Jesus.

A Learning Process

To be sure, building family in a singles' household isn't easy. It isn't something most people come into the kingdom of God knowing how to do. Many have not had a positive home experience themselves and have no clue how to build a sense of family. This is something that needs to be taught and learned. I'm 32 years old and have lived in many singles' households over the past nine years. In some we have experienced family and in some we haven't. The difference between those that have been a success and those that have not is simply a *decision* that we would work to make our living situation a family. We started out with a family devotional on household expectations and came up with ideas on how we all wanted to participate to build a family. (This is also important when a new roommate moves into an already existing household.) Some of the issues we discussed were as follows:

- which night of the week we would have our family devotional
- what time of day we would all pray together
- who would be responsible for handling which utility bills
- how we would handle the chores
- how we would purchase groceries (together or separately)
- how we would handle cooking meals

In addition, we set up expectations such as the following:

- If you are not coming home at night, call and let someone know.
- Do chores weekly.
- Pay bills on time.
- Do not leave dishes in the sink at night.
- Pick up the living room before bed.
- Tell roommates if someone is coming over to spend the night or to eat a meal.
- Be open about anything that bothers you in the household.

These have been just a few expectations, and during the course of time different households have had to talk through what works and doesn't work. With the common foundation of family, we have been able to work through bumps more quickly, to have open and honest relationships and to have a household that is peaceful and also a lot of fun.

Stay with It

In one of my living situations, one roommate consistently had a hard time getting home on time for our once-a-week family devotionals. Her heart simply was not into what we were trying to build. We had talked often during the year about why building family was important. She had other activities that took priority over her getting home or that prompted her to ask us to reschedule. She also felt like our times together weren't fun.

After talking, having fun together, and getting much advice from others, her heart still didn't change. She still felt as if her ministry activities were more important. What she needed to realize was that the family we were trying to build was a part of her ministry. There will always be other needs around us in our ministry groups. If we don't make these times special and devote our hearts to them, building family will not "just happen." (Since then, I'm delighted to say, she has really changed and now comes home on time, ready to give to everyone.)

Conflict resolution is a vital part of "family life." It is virtually impossible to live with anyone and not have conflicts arise (even when you are married to the man or woman you love with all your heart!). Too many times roommates have left things unsaid and unforgiven. Ephesians 4:26 instructs us, "In your anger do not sin": Do not let the sun go down while you are still angry." Even though the desire to leave things unresolved may be there, it is right to work out your differences and to do it quickly. My roommate and I were able to resolve the "disaster" conflict mentioned at the beginning of the chapter because we both wanted to do what was right. We also both reflected on our family agreements and remembered Jesus' call to consider others' needs above our own.

Getting Specific

I want to share about a few of the times we've had that have been really enjoyable. We've had dinners by candlelight, lessons from the Scriptures, piano playing, practicing singing new spiritual songs, canoe rides, walks in the woods, card games, reading each other favorite bedtime stories or poetry, movie nights, and times with others who joined us. These times together have made the difference for us. They have made us more than individuals; they have made us family.

The following scripture reminds me that all the effort and hard work are worth it:

> *Finally, all of you, live in harmony with one another; be sympathetic, love as brothers, be compassionate and humble. Do not repay evil with evil or insult with insult, but with blessing, because to this you were called so that you may inherit a blessing (1 Peter 3:8-9).*

I can honestly say my roommates are my best friends. We truly love each other and love being together. We love coming home at the end of a long day, praying together and being there for each other—no matter what we may be going through. We are emotionally connected, but not possessive of each other. We are close, but none of us feels smothered. I believe we have something the world could never offer—something that really shines like a beacon to the lost world and brings glory to God.

Part III

❦

·HOSPITALITY·

· A Biblical Understanding ·

❦

Practice hospitality.

ROMANS 12:13

For everything that was written
in the past was written to teach us, so that
through endurance and the encouragement
of the scriptures we might have hope.

ROMANS 15:4

CHAPTER 9

God's Word on the Matter

KAY McKEAN

"In the beginning God created the heavens and the earth." The first words of the Bible describe for us how God took nothing, and out of that nothing he created something: a home for mankind. Our home, planet Earth, was created by God to become an environment that would be beautiful for his people, that would sustain them so that they could live and work and raise families, and so that they could glorify and worship God.

The first ones to be given this home were Adam and Eve. God commanded them to live in their home, the Garden of Eden, and also to do the work that God gave them to do: to give names to all the creatures that God had created. Other players in God's drama were also given homes. Noah's home was the ark, where he was to be host, not only to human beings, but also to animals so that they would be protected from the flood. Abraham's traveling home was a tent, from which he entertained heavenly visitors. The Israelites were given a home, a land of their own, where centuries later, the Messiah would be born. Whatever the location or type of dwelling, homes were always intended to be a place from which the work of God would be accomplished.

God Blesses Hospitality

The home was also a means through which God could bless his people. After Abraham's hospitality toward his three visitors, he was promised a son. Lot's home was opened to angels who ultimately secured his escape from the destruction of Sodom and Gomorrah. Rebekah invited Abraham's servant to her family's home, and got a husband in the bargain! The widow of Zaraphath provided housing for Elijah, and survived a famine because of it. A Shunammite woman built a room onto her house for Elisha, and was blessed with a son. Esther prepared a palace feast, and saved her people from destruction.

As history marched forward to the time of Christ, we see that God was still using homes to bring him glory, regardless of the type of dwelling they might have been. God took a shelter for animals and made it into the birthplace of the Savior of the world. The homes of "sinners" and "tax collectors" became catalysts for repentance and beacons of hope. God used the homes of Jews and Gentiles, men and women, jailers and prominent citizens to advance his kingdom following the days of Pentecost.

Our Father continues to use homes as places where the saved can be refreshed and the good news can be preached to the lost. Bible studies, church services and reviving devotionals have been presented in living rooms, dormitory rooms and kitchens across the world. Whatever the dwelling may be (a boat, a cave, a hut, a tent, a cottage, a palace or a suburban ranch with two-car garage), God can use it to further his cause, *if* the inhabitants are surrendered to doing his will.

Drawing Close to God

Jesus and his followers demonstrate the incredible blessings that can occur when the home is used as a place to draw closer to God. Jesus himself did not have a home to call his own, as he reminds us in Matthew 8:20, "Foxes have holes and birds of the air have nests, but the Son of Man has no place to lay his head." However, this did not stop him from showing the blessings of hospitality, even if it was in another person's home! Each time Jesus was invited, or invited himself, into someone's home, the residents were able to either receive or to witness healing, salvation, and the very words of life. Think on the numerous examples of this: Zacchaeus the tax collector radically repented following a meal in his home with Jesus (Luke 19:5-8); a lesson on love and forgiveness was delivered and exhibited in a Pharisee's home (Luke 7:36-50); a visit to Martha's home led to a reminder of what was truly best and most important (Luke 10:38-42); Jesus' anointing and his commendation of a woman's love took place during a meal at Simon's home (Mark 14:3-9); a paralytic was forgiven and healed after he and his friends "crashed" a gathering in Capernaum (Mark 2:1-12); Jesus sent out the mission team of seventy-two, telling them to enter homes and to eat and drink what they were given (Matthew 10:7). These are only a few of the instances where the home is mentioned as the venue for the work of God. Surely God is deliberately showing us the incredible ways that he can be glorified through the opening of homes.

The Early Church

In the infancy of the church, it is not surprising to see the early disciples walking the same path of hospitality and thereby advancing the kingdom in so many ways. The church was meeting together daily as they "broke bread in their homes and ate together with glad and sincere hearts" (Acts 2:46). The ministry to the Gentiles began in Cornelius' home (Acts 10:25ff). A prayer group, meeting at Mary's house, received Peter after his miraculous escape from prison (Acts 12:12). Paul's ministry in Philippi was headquartered in the home of Lydia, his first convert there (Acts 16:13-15). The Philippian jailer prepared a meal for Paul and Silas in his home following his baptism (Acts 16:31-34). Priscilla and Aquila were hosts to Paul in Corinth, and later to Apollos in Ephesus (Acts 18:3, 26). The recorded *Acts of the Apostles* closes out with the message of hospitality: "For two whole years Paul stayed there *in his own rented house* and welcomed all who came to see him. Boldly and without hindrance he preached the kingdom of God and taught about the Lord Jesus Christ" (Acts 28:30-31, emphasis added).

The letters to the early Christians show the importance and necessity of homes being used to serve God. The church met at the home of Priscilla and Aquila in Rome (Romans 16:3-5) and in the home of Nympha in Colosse (Colossians 4:15). Paul and the whole church enjoyed the hospitality of Gaius (Romans 16:23). Paul asked Philemon to welcome Onesimus, and also to prepare a guest room for himself (Philemon 17-22). The Bible makes it clear that Christian hospitality was vital to the spread of the gospel and the growth of the church!

Commands and Examples

The term "cocooning" has been used recently to indicate the isolating of a person or family in order to survive these uncertain and tumultuous times. It is understandable to want to lock our doors, pull down the shades and keep to ourselves for safety and security. But when we have an "us four no more" mentality, not only do we deny others a chance to have their needs met, we also deny ourselves the opportunity to enjoy the blessings of sharing with others. Romans 12:13 is not just a suggestion, but a command from God for us to fulfill his purpose for our lives: "Share with God's people who are in need. Practice hospitality."

Unconditional. Hospitality is not limited to inviting into our homes people who are just like us. Jesus condemned this action in Luke 14:13: "When you give a banquet, invite the poor, the crippled, the lame, the blind, and you will be blessed." Many people open their homes only to people with whom they feel naturally comfortable. Clearly the directive is to open our homes to all types of people in order to serve and share with them all. In this way, we have the added benefit of learning about people from all walks of life: We are able to learn from people of different races, cultures and backgrounds.

Unselfish. Hospitality is not a means to popularity or selfish gain, as Jesus goes on to say in Luke 14:14, "Although they cannot repay you, you will be repaid at the resurrection of the righteous." We see that Jesus' idea of hospitality is not simply to entertain, to impress, to get a promotion or to get ahead, but to *give.* Any other attitude will not bring about the blessings that God has promised.

Compassionate. One of the greatest aspects of hospitality is having the opportunity to meet the needs of others. In Matthew 25: 31-45, we learn that as we feed, clothe, visit, look after and invite in others, it is as if we are doing so for Jesus himself! Our hospitality cannot be a self-serving agenda, designed to make ourselves feel good, but rather, a way to learn how to understand, serve and love other people.

Joyful. A very specific reminder is given to us in 1 Peter 4:9: "Offer hospitality to one another without grumbling." It is ludicrous to consider the possibility of having someone into your home and expecting them to feel comfortable if you are muttering and scowling, reminding them of how much trouble it is! While few would actually go that far, guests can sense tension, anxiety and exasperation, even if we are trying to hide it. On the contrary, our visitors should sense our thankfulness and joy that they have come to visit us!

Quality. The wedding at Cana gave Jesus the opportunity to serve by turning water into wine. This wasn't just watery wine, but was, as we see in John 2:10, "the best wine." God's habit of always giving the best is the example we must follow as we are serving others in our homes. Throughout Scripture we see that hospitality was not displayed in a sloppy, uncaring way, but with great attention and care. What a wonderful opportunity for us to deny ourselves and give the best we have for the benefit of others.

Prepared. Perhaps one of the most encouraging passages in the Bible is Jesus' statement, found in John 14:2, that he would go and "prepare a place" for us in his Father's house. To be hospitable does require some planning and effort. Although our homes should be open at all times to others, there is a need for disciples to work and prepare for guests who are expected. Waiting until the last moment to receive people into our homes indicates a lack of concern and respect. When we know guests are coming, we should do all we can to let them know we have looked forward to their arrival and have done all we can do to make them feel welcome.

Following the Example

God's kingdom must advance, and we as 20th-century disciples will have a great hand in that advancement as we obey the command to be hospitable. As I read in the Bible of souls being saved through hospitality, I am reminded of so many stories of conversions in recent years that began with the question, "Would you like to come to my home?" As those in our modern world become more and more isolated from one another, we are exhorted to be different and to open our homes to the lost and to the saved.

Hospitality may come naturally to some people, while others have to work at it more. We can all be encouraged and challenged by men and women who have left their own familiar culture and country and have learned how to be hospitable in a foreign land, often in a foreign language. Missionaries around the world must learn how to make a home in an unfamiliar environment and use that home to further the kingdom of God. I am personally inspired by the women who have learned new ways to shop, cook, serve and speak so that they can help others know God. These are great examples to us of modern-day hospitality, and we must strive to imitate their hearts and their actions.

The Host with the Most

God is our ultimate example of hospitality. He has provided a home for us on this earth, a place to live and work and do his will. He has welcomed us into his kingdom and provided us with a sustaining environment, the church. The church, the people of God, is like a home. It provides security; it is a haven, a safe place. It is not a place to hide, but rather, supplies the courage to go out into the world and help others. The head of this "home" is Jesus himself, and he leads his family to incredible blessings.

Finally, God protects us in the church until we go to be with him forever in our eternal home. The scriptures that describe heaven for us speak of feasts and banquets, of weddings, of beautiful places, of joy, of celebration—all the things that are considered lovely in this world. I believe that God knows we can't fathom how wonderful heaven will be, but he gives us enough clues to know that it will be awesome! What is even better is that God will be there to welcome us! To give us the privilege to go to heaven is the greatest act of hospitality we will ever experience!

Gaius, whose hospitality
I and the whole church here enjoy,
sends you his greetings.

ROMANS 16:23

CHAPTER 10

Not for Women Only

RON BRUMLEY

The statistics are not in yet, but I imagine that, after perusing the Table of Contents of this book, the majority of readers will be women. Quite honestly, if I hadn't been asked to participate in the writing of it, I probably wouldn't have purchased a copy either. (Actually, I'm hoping to receive a free one for my efforts.) My point is that men often leave "hospitality" up to their wives—the same men who believe in 1 Timothy 3:2 and in Titus 1:8 that says "the overseer must be...hospitable." This quality of character that elders are to exhibit is addressed to the elder—not the wives of elders. This truth must attract our attention, men, and elicit our obedience.

Certainly, some men are more blessed with the gift of serving, which includes being hospitable. But as with most gifts from God, the exercise of them brings about growth and maturity. It is my firm conviction that all male disciples can and need to grow in the gift of serving—of being hospitable as we reach out and influence the fragmented world in which we live. For elders, and those who have their hearts set on being an elder, God says we must be hospitable. So men, let's read and study and grow in our hospitality. It's definitely a subject *not for women only*.

To start with, a good working definition of hospitality is having the heart and making the effort to meet the needs of other people, family, friends and strangers. Our focus here is the expression of hospitality as practiced in our homes. All people have the need to feel warmly loved and included. All of us have the need to feel enjoyed, appreciated and included into a family. Our homes, apartments, town houses, condos and all our belongings are gifts to us from our generous and loving heavenly Father, who intends for us to use them to further his purposes. All the wonderful blessings and gifts we receive from God can be either a tremendous asset in our expression of hospitality, or a huge stumbling block as we consume ourselves in fulfilling our own pleasures and comforts.

Hospitality goes beyond the courtesy of rising and greeting people as they enter our home (though this is important). It goes beyond preparing and sharing a meal with others (though this, too, is important). Hospitality is about communicating in a variety of ways the great lengths we have gone to in order to make the time with our guests special—that we've organized everything and set the tone and atmosphere with them in mind. By our interest in them and our conversation that draws them out, they clearly sense that they are our focus for the evening.

Married Disciples

To accomplish this level of hospitality requires a team effort, with both husband and wife working together to achieve the goal. Linda and I make it a practice to both answer the door and greet our guests upon their arrival. Before this, while Linda is preparing the meal (I know my limitations), I take care of last-minute details that are important to both of us (running the vacuum one last time, straightening the pillows on the sofa, selecting appropriate music, organizing the magazines on the coffee table or checking the comfort level of the temperature in the room). If children are included in the evening (which we encourage—we're trying to build a feeling of family), we arrange our small, child-sized table and chairs and prepare for their use. As my talented wife, who has become so after many years of faithful practice, puts the finishing touches on a well-planned and delicious meal, I take drink orders, fill glasses with ice, pour coffee and generally act the host. If additional items are needed after being seated at the tables, I will as likely go after them as Linda. When our guests arrive, and as they share a meal with us, we want them to walk into an environment that has obviously been pre-planned and arranged with their needs and comforts in mind.

There are several forces working against modern-day men in achieving the level of hospitality that God expects. For one, most of us haven't been trained by our parents or by society to think this way. Etiquette is thought to be a relic of some past civilization. In actuality, etiquette is a set of guidelines that define courtesy. Surely we can go overboard with rules and guidelines of proper social behavior, but being a gracious host, showing courtesy and respect through our hospitality is a vivid display of the kind of love that is "not rude" (1 Corinthians 13:5).

Another inhibiting factor keeping the grace of hospitality from being practiced to its zenith, especially by the male gender, is a misapplication of Acts 6. For leaders to "neglect the ministry" to "wait on tables" is not a warning against being hospitable. The Bible does *not* contradict itself. For an elder, evangelist or other leader to run a program as time-consuming as "daily distributing food" would be a misuse of talents and the wrong focus for leaders, and would serve to deprive others equally qualified of the opportunity to serve. I believe that there is a danger of overextending the application of this verse, however, whereby leaders (even leaders of families) could wrongly conclude that their role is not to serve tables in any fashion. Remember, an elder "must be hospitable."

In general, I believe men must constantly strive to overcome the sin of self-centeredness. This sin causes a variety of problems for us and can certainly limit our growth in being hospitable. A heart that is set on protecting one's leisure time, recreation time, private time, family-alone time, is not a heart that is striving to excel in the grace of hospitality. For sure it is vital that we plan time to be alone—with God, with our spouse and our family. But the heart of a hospitable man is looking forward to and planning for times to meet the needs of others as well.

A Few Thoughts for Singles

Both of our sons have lived in multiple-roommate situations while in college. I do believe these experiences provided additional motivation to both to be married early. (In the case of our youngest son, to *want* to be married soon—at this writing, he's definitely a wanna-be).

Their mom did what she could to help the boys and their roommates to present their living quarters in an attractive and hospitable style. Living together with two to three guys is no one's idea of a permanent lifestyle. But, there are decisions that need to be made and standards that need to be agreed upon to make even single guys' living quarters inviting.

It begins with everyone deciding that the current arrangement is to be enjoyed instead of seeing it as a temporary, less-than-ideal holding pattern that must be endured. With that frame of mind, disorder, dust, depression and disgust are bound to reign—hardly an atmosphere in which to "practice hospitality" (Romans 12:13). Most households of guys I've ever seen, and I've seen a bunch, could use a generous amount of the feminine touch. This can happen without the guys having to become feminine themselves (a great relief to all, I'm sure!). My suggestion is to find a mom of older teen guys—perhaps one whose own boys have moved out. She will be a wellspring of ideas and assistance to bring order, good odors and ocular delights to the fore. This verse must have been written with single guys' households in mind: "Offer hospitality to one another without grumbling" (1 Peter 4:9). If you get the right kind of help and decide to change the way you live, your living arrangement can be a pleasant environment, conducive to "offering hospitality."

NOT
FOR
WOMEN
ONLY

Men, as one of the older guys in the kingdom leadership pool, I encourage you to read this entire book and provide leadership in the area of being hospitable. It is a teaching addressed to all of us and is a tremendous tool to help us share God's love with others.

CHAPTER 11

Impact for Evangelism

KIM STRONDAK

"I've met some Christians who live down the street. They want us to come to dinner," said my live-in boyfriend ten years ago and before I was a disciple.

"No way! I won't have anything in common with them. I'm sure they're boring and unrelatable."

I imagined these "Christians" to be uneducated, overweight and anything but fun! Pictures of my neighbors as a child came to mind: women who wouldn't wear makeup, couldn't cut their hair or wear pants, and kids who weren't allowed to participate in gym class, go bowling or play cards.

I must have eventually said yes to dinner because two weeks later I found myself in the home of my Christian neighbors Fred and Ellen Faller, and I remember the impressions of that first evening as if it were yesterday. What a surprise! Their home was very warm and inviting, yet simply decorated. As I stood in the dining room, my eyes roamed from the clean hardwood floors to the crisp country curtains and then down the rungs of the ladder-backed chairs on which Fred had carved hearts and flowers for Ellen. Then my gaze came to rest on the center of attention for the evening, their beautifully decorated dining room table, covered with a blue calico tablecloth along with matching cloth napkins. Two candles flickered in the center. Ellen had filled her blue and white place settings with warm bread, tossed salad with raisins and shaved carrots on top and a delicious haddock casserole.

With each forkful of food, the thick calluses on my heart began to soften as the Faller's home and hospitality impacted my very soul. *How could these people be Christians?* I thought, *I am having so much fun!* Fred had us all laughing as he told one story after another. Ellen was very friendly and gracious. She was happy to have us in her home and was very interested in the things I liked to do. The evening flew by quickly, and as I stood in the doorway to say good night to my new friends, I thought to myself, *I loved tonight. I hope they'll invite me to come back soon.*

Because of the Faller's home and continued hospitality, I was attracted to God's kingdom. I asked Ellen, "What makes you tick?"

She replied, "God and his Word. Would you like to study the Bible with me?"

Without hesitation I answered, "Yes!"

However, shortly after that talk I moved to northern Massachusetts. I started to study the Bible with some single women there. One of them invited me over for dinner. I walked into a dark, sparsely decorated and gloomily lit apartment. As we sat down at a small table in the kitchen, she cleaned off its top with a swipe of her arm and then added breakfast's dirty dishes to the heap already in the sink. Her hospitality included a spoon and a bowl of pasta plunked in front of me. Her conversation was minimal, and it appeared we didn't have much in common. My heart sank. When these disciples didn't turn up their heat in the winter, didn't share their food or decorate for the holidays, I thought back to Ellen's home and remembered that not all disciples are like this. Had I met these women first, I believe their lack of hospitality and their home's lack of warmth and friendliness would have really turned me off to their message; I didn't want to be like them.

In the preceding chapter, Kay did a great job of presenting a common thread that weaves through both the Old and New Testaments. That thread is hospitality! Almost every conversion in the New Testament is accompanied by an act of hospitality, and as modern disciples, God continues to weave that thread into our lives and homes as we reach out to our friends, family and neighbors in a lost world.

You may ask, "How can I make an impact in my neighborhood?" "How can I turn a perfect stranger into my new best friend?" "How can I win souls and be abundantly fruitful?" Your home is one of the most important avenues for evangelism that God has given you. Looking back over the past ten years of being a disciple, I realized that every new friend I've made, every soul I have helped to convert and the ministry I have helped to build have been affected by time around my dinner table. Brunches, luncheons, dinner parties, pizza extravaganzas, campus turkey dinners, chili and "chowda" fests, Sunday BBQs, birthday parties, wine and cheese parties, chocolate parties and jam-making gatherings are some of the fond and fun memories of the hospitable ways I've used my home to win hearts and souls for Jesus.

Displaying God's Love

Count the number of times that you have been invited to dinner by a neighbor, a coworker or an acquaintance whom you did not invite to your home first. The occasions are rare today. In all my neighborhoods,

I have been the initiator, the one who said hello first, the one who knocked on the door to meet the neighbors. So often I've wished it were the other way around, but I've learned that extending hospitality as a disciple is a powerful way for me to show God's love to others. As I deliver cookies to my neighbor or invite her over to make homemade jam, I remember that God initiated with me first. He had Jesus die for me when I didn't even care, and he continued to patiently and unconditionally reach out to me until I finally responded and let him win my heart.

Opening our homes and extending our love and hospitality must characterize our lifestyles as disciples. It is not a method to bring quick fruit, not another task to add to our "To Do" lists, but instead, it needs to be part of our character. It needs to be what we are known for in our neighborhoods and workplaces. The apostle Paul in Romans 12:1 says to each of us as disciples, "in view of God's mercy...offer your bodies as living sacrifices, holy and pleasing to God—this is your spiritual act of worship." He then goes on to give specifics of how to offer our bodies; in Romans 12:13 he says, "Practice hospitality." What a powerful display of God's love your dinner guest sees as you share your home and your food, asking nothing in return. What a sharp contrast to the usual mindset of "I'll do this if there is something in it for me," i.e. a promotion, a sales pitch or a return favor!

A Glimpse of God's Church

As disciples our homes are microcosms of God's church. Our homes on a small scale display the warmth, friendliness, servanthood, love, harmony and order of the body of Christ. A friend of mine asked her neighbor who had just become a Christian, "Why did you keep studying the Bible with me while you were being pulled in another direction by other people in your life?" Nancy replied, "Because of your home and your life. You are really living out what you teach, and your life is very attractive to me."

Our homes are extensions of ourselves and reflect our priorities and convictions. Your guests make decisions from their time spent with you as to whether they want to become more involved with you and with spiritual pursuits. Just as when we want our worship services and spiritual events to be excellent in order to reflect God's excellence, we as homemakers need to strive for excellence in our homes and in our hospitality. The Scriptures remind us, "Watch your life and doctrine closely. Persevere in them, because if you do, you will save both yourself and your hearers"(1 Timothy 4:16). Larry and I have had many people turn down our initial invitation to church only to subsequently accept after coming to dinner. One man said he was going to come to our church from now on because he had never had the minister and his wife from any church personally invite him over for a home-cooked meal. (He really liked the BBQ chicken wings!)

Turning Hearts to God

"Let us not become weary in doing good, for at the proper time, we will reap a harvest if we do not give up. Therefore, as we have opportunity, let us do good to all people" (Galatians 6:9-10).

As you practice hospitality as a lifestyle, the Scriptures teach that you will reap a harvest at the proper time if you do not give up. I have heard countless stories of neighbors becoming Christians two or three years after they were initially met because they were impacted through those years by the difference in the lives of the disciples. Have you given up hope for your neighborhood, declaring, "No one is open. I've shared with them all"? What is your attitude about your workplace? Are you hospitable even though no one is visibly responding?

Twenty years ago in Boston, Gloria Baird was hospitable to a woman named Helen, who had young children. Gloria shared her life and the gospel with Helen, who at that time did not become a disciple. Fifteen years later her two daughters became disciples. Over the years Helen and her husband never forgot the seeds that had been planted by the Bairds as they had extended their hospitality to them. Several years later they both became disciples! Never underestimate the power of hospitality. When singles are being unproductive and unfruitful in their ministries, I ask them about their hospitality. One frustrated single disciple moaned that she didn't have time to have anyone over for dinner. Her dinners consisted of "McFood" from the drive-thru on the way home from work as she was on her way to study the Bible with a friend. I told her she was not going to win souls that way. Someone might be turned on to the gospel, but be turned off by her frenzied lifestyle. She learned to use her home to share her life and the gospel instead of running from here to there. She became happy and fruitful.

As I walk through the fellowship and look at the faces of disciples whose lives have been impacted for God by my dinner table and by the Strondak family's hospitality, I smile. God is so good in giving us the fulfilling purpose of winning souls for him and having lots of fun while we're at it by practicing hospitality!

·The Neighborhood·

In 1987 we were moving from the large house in which we had raised our family to a small house in a new neighborhood. We were eager for the opportunity to reach out to new neighbors.

Many early mornings before construction crews arrived, I drove to the new neighborhood and walked the block praying for the families who would move into the houses. I stood in our newly framed house one morning—no windows, no doors—and asked God that our home would always seem that open to our neighbors.

As my two youngest children were high school students, I didn't have a natural link to the younger families in that neighborhood. So I went to garage sales and collected inexpensive toys that I stored in an under-bed box in my bedroom. Before long, most neighborhood kids knew where to find the toys when they visited. I purchased kid videos to entertain my young guests.

I made Thursday afternoons my "neighborhood day." On that day I would pay drop-in visits to neighbors to get to know them better. I kept my ear closely attuned to needs. I found a young widowed mother who needed a friend and confidante. I found a young mother whose baby had a heart condition and could only be left with trained baby-sitters. My 16-year-old daughter and I learned infant CPR so we could be her relief. I volunteered for house-sitting while people were on vacation. I used every opportunity I could think of to deliver goodies: pumpkin muffins at Thanksgiving with notes saying we were thankful for our neighbors, pecan butter and muffin mixes at Christmas, heart-shaped cookies on Valentine's Day with notes to say "We love you."

We bought a front yard bench and used it as often as possible to be visible and to catch passers by for conversation.

Word got out (on purpose) among the neighborhood kids that my cookie jar was always full and that they could help with the baking on Thursdays after school...with a strong probability they could go home with platters for their families.

We only lived in that house for two and a half years, but five of our neighbors became disciples in that time. We not only loved our neighbors, but we helped them to love each other.

Linda Brumley

· Response to Outreach ·

As we arrived at Ron and Linda Brumley's home for dinner that evening fifteen years ago, I never expected that my life was going to be so profoundly impacted. When Ron opened the door, we entered the warmest, friendliest home I had ever seen. All four of their children were there to greet us enthusiastically before we were ushered into their living room. It contained pictures of several decades of relatives, as well as many different antiques and other interesting paraphernalia, all of which helped give their home a distinct personality.

There were happy, joyful sounds coming from the kitchen as Linda and her daughters, Meredith and Gretchen, prepared the meal. The emanating aroma soon had my mouth watering in anticipation for what promised to be a delightful meal.

As we sat down for a sumptuous candlelight dinner, I was immediately impressed by the place cards the children had made. I quickly became overwhelmed by the love and respect each member of the Brumley family had for one another. There was no petty quarreling between siblings; in fact, all of the kids actually enjoyed conversing with each other. I was even more dumbfounded when their oldest son, Greg, asked his sister Meredith to get him another helping of food and she readily agreed. I never believed this type of relationship could exist between a brother and sister! As I continued to stare at this amazing family, I found my appetite quickly vanishing as I caught a vision of what I wanted my family to one day become—godly.

After dinner, we retired to the family room and participated in a family devotional which inspired me even more and gave me hope that it is possible to raise awesome kids even in today's turbulent society.

As we drove home that evening, my wife, Shelley, and I were so excited and convicted that we couldn't stop talking about what we had just experienced. After we became disciples, that evening became a model for what our family was to become in the years ahead. And, as people have visited our home and been impressed by our family, I always like to mention what God showed us that night at the Brumley home. Surely God does draw people into his family as we share our own family with others.

Greg Metten

CHAPTER 12

Encourage One Another

SHEILA JONES

As is true with many other families of five or more, we have had people into our home more than we have been invited to others' homes. But one such invitation stands out in my mind. Several years ago, before any of our three girls had gone off to college, Mike and Janet Hammonds invited us over for dinner. I was thrilled! I did not have to cook...somebody else was going to do it.

After being warmly welcomed into their home, I was overcome with gratitude when we sat down to eat an incredible home-cooked meal: grilled chicken, corn, and other yummy things. I kept thinking, *I can't believe someone would care enough to go to all this trouble for us.*

That night helped me to realize how powerful and encouraging the practice of hospitality really is. I knew more about what people felt when I invited them over for a meal at my home—especially if they had a large family with any teenagers.

What a right and godly way to show people God's love. He was willing to be inconvenienced for us, to give of himself in the deepest way possible. Certainly, he did not just cook a meal; he sacrificed his Son. But when we give unselfishly to people without expecting or requiring that they give back to us, we are showing the nature of his heart.

Being true to his compassionate, hospitable nature, God encouraged and strengthened his tired and discouraged prophet by sending an angel to bake bread for him and to give him water (1 Kings 19:1-9). He calls us as brothers and sisters to imitate him by strengthening and encouraging each other. Paul says,

> *Let us not become weary in doing good, for at the proper time we will reap a harvest if we do not give up. Therefore, as we have opportunity, let us do good to all people, especially to those who belong to the family of believers (Galatians 6:9-10).*

As disciples, we can sometimes have the mind-set of giving our best to nondisciples because we want them to come to know God, but then not take the time or energy to give to our brothers and sisters. As Paul says, we must do good to all people, but we must especially do good to those who are our siblings in the family of believers. In fact, Peter's injunction to "offer hospitality to one another without grumbling" is written to a group of Christians (1 Peter 4:9).

Ask yourself the following questions and then read about the encouragement from other Christians received by a young college student and a married couple:

- How often do I invite Christian friends over for a meal?
- Do I take for granted those who are closest to me, or do I take opportunities to show them how special they are to me?
- When have I invited a leader and his/her family over to honor them for their unselfish service? Do I just assume they are too busy and never ask?
- Have I allowed myself to become "weary in doing good" to my brothers and sisters?

College Student

BETTY DYSON

Many years ago, a college student who lived in a dorm far from home became a disciple. Her parents, brothers and sisters did not understand her new commitment to God.

College life was very challenging. Every year there were moves to different dorms and the difficulty of quickly making new friends. Even the challenge of facing "mystery meat" in the dorm cafeteria was depressing. This student loved to cook, but she never had an opportunity to do that at college.

I will never forget being this new Christian in college. I felt the emotional distance from my family and began to wonder about the commitment I had made. *Is this just a college thing? What will happen to my love for God when I get out of college?*

Soon afterwards, God sent an older woman into my life. She reached out to me one day in fellowship, and we had a great talk about our lives. She was very interested in me, my background and my activities as a student. She suggested meeting me for lunch near campus. After a while, we began meeting for lunch at least two or three times a month.

My friend also invited me into her home. We cooked many meals together, and I remember watching her whole family. Her children were happy and very giving. It was obvious that their father loved them deeply. We all had such great times together as we ate dinner, talked and laughed.

I remember the day my heart changed. My doubts and fears about my commitment subsided. I knew that what I was experiencing was real. This family and their home was what God intended family and home to be. I was filled with gratitude for the blessings I had in God's kingdom. Hope filled my heart as I thought of the family I could have one day.

Twenty-one years later, I look back on all of those wonderful memories of hospitality extended to me, a young Christian. I thank God, because I don't believe I would have remained faithful if I had not been loved so deeply by a Christian family who showed God's heart to me. Their lives made it clear to me that the peace and purpose I had experienced as a college student was something that would stay with me for a lifetime if I stayed with God. Praise God for a faithful couple who practiced hospitality from their hearts as God commanded!

Young Married Couple

THOMAS AND GILLIAN NOLTE

To tell you the truth, what really helped Gillian and me not only to become disciples, but also to grow in our love and gratitude for people in general was the warmth in friendship and hospitality shown to us by Joe and Carolyn Fields as we were studying the Bible. (We practically lived in their house, ate all their food, swam in their pool, played with the kids....) Later we received the same loving care from Tom and Janet Arnett in their house in Coronado.

Whenever we were invited (or invited ourselves), there was an abundance of joy, fun, food, visitors, activities and more in store for us, combined with an openness and love that made us feel a part of their family at all times. Whether we were cooking together, watching a movie, cleaning up the pool area or sitting in the jacuzzi—all of these activities showed us God's love.

We learned so much from all of them in that time. Their understanding, giving and sharing was not a means to an end; it was a lifestyle. We knew that no matter what happened, we could always count on them to provide for us an accepting and joy-filled environment.

On top of all that, God allowed us one afternoon with the Fields, the Arnetts, another couple and my parents, who had come from Germany to visit us in San Diego. We arranged a special southern meal, cooking together, laughing and talking as we all enjoyed this special time. It showed my parents that love is real in God's church, that the people are real and love to serve one another. Ever since that day, my parents have given up their reservations about our commitment to the point of now defending us when others are critical.

This is for us a great encouragement as we have now moved very close to my parents in Germany. We, along with others, have started a new church to show more people that John 13:34-35 really comes alive in true hospitality in our homes!

· Attitudes of Hospitality ·

Offer hospitality to
one another without grumbling.

1 PETER 4:9

A generous man will prosper;
he who refreshes others will
himself be refreshed.

PROVERBS 11:25

CHAPTER 13

Eager, Not Just Willing

LINDA BRUMLEY

Three or four years into our marriage, I found myself still resisting my husband's magnanimous open-door policy, for which I was ill-equipped both by temperament and by talent. I preferred solitude to company. I was a novice cook, an up-tight perfectionist and a penny-pincher on a limited budget.

Ron's generous invitations were frequent. Extended to both friends and strangers, singles and families, his offer could be for coffee and dessert or for several weeks' stay with three meals a day and laundry privileges. Sometimes these ideas were discussed in advance and sometimes not.

I was religious and a Bible reader, but I had either not noticed or not comprehended the command to "offer hospitality to one another without grumbling" (1 Peter 4:9). I did not offer—my husband did. What I did was grumble!

One day while reading Romans 12:6-8, I was deep in thought about the various gifts God gave to people. Reading on in Romans 12:13, I found a two word command: "Practice hospitality." It occurred to me that if hospitality had been listed as a spiritual gift, it was surely the one that God had given to Ron! (Certainly one application of the gift of serving would be hospitality.)

I realized with startling clarity that I did not want to stand before God and account for how I had taken the amazing blessing he had given my husband and had systematically destroyed it. I made a firm decision to change and immediately became a student of the art of hospitality. I pondered the woman in 2 Kings 4:8-10 who anticipated the needs of her guest, Elisha, and prepared to meet them—even to furnishing an add-on room. I noted that she and Lydia (Acts 16:14-15) both "urged" and "persuaded" their guests to accept their hospitality. My selfishness was exposed! My heart needed to become *eager*, not just *willing*.

In others' homes I took mental notes of the things that made me feel welcome. I collected a few simple, inexpensive, yet attractive and tasty, main dish recipes and became accomplished at them. One chicken dish in particular would elicit the "Who's coming to dinner?" question from my children.

Because of Ron's frequent spontaneous invitations, I learned to keep certain ingredients on hand to accommodate sudden full spreads.

I learned to arrange furniture cozily for good conversation. I learned when it was smart to sit around a table and when a buffet was more advantageous. I learned that a pretty table makes a simple meal seem like more than it is and that a wise hostess has a specialty. Initially mine was homemade bread; served with peasant soup and gingham napkins, it seemed like a great feast. And it was cheap! I learned that meals prepared in advance made me a calmer hostess.

I collected gingham napkins, made by my nearly blind grandmother during a visit of several weeks. In preparing for her stay, I tried to find handwork projects that could be accomplished even with dim vision. I bought yards and yards of gingham, a fabric that lends itself to fringing. She loved it! And I still have close to one hundred of them, born *of* hospitality and used *for* hospitality.

During this early focus on hospitality, we were privileged to build our own home. Ron and I prayed together often during its construction that we would remember that it belonged to Jesus and not us. We lived in that house for fifteen years; only three of which found us living alone with our family. We rearranged constantly to make room for others. Our children were accustomed to giving up their beds and sharing their toys. Ron routinely cleared out the garage to store other people's possessions.

One night, Ron and I were visiting Kathy, a troubled fifteen-year-old, at the hospital. The aftermath of Kathy's suicide attempt revealed that her stepfather was sexually abusing her. Kathy's mother and the psychiatrist were discussing her release from the hospital, while Kathy, making eye contact only with a spot on the floor, assured us that she would run away or kill herself if returned to her home. The statement did not move the psychiatrist to reevaluate his decision to release her the following day. Then I heard my husband say, "Kathy can come stay with us." This offer was met with enthusiasm by her mother and the doctor. I joined Kathy in her contemplation of the spot on the floor.

I kept expecting someone to realize it was a bad idea. I felt angry with Ron for offering. I despised my reluctance compared to his compassion. I tried to determine if the intense fear I felt was rational or hysterical, if God was asking me to take Kathy or if we were asking for trouble. I battled against the memory of our prayers vowing that we would share our house freely. Kathy came the next day and shared a room with our five- and ten-year-old daughters for two months. The story did not end with a victory for Kathy, but it was a victory for me and for my daughters. I had allowed God to dig much deeper in my heart to uncover selfishness, hysterical fear and a silent critical bitterness toward my husband. I became more faithful, more joyfully submissive, more a partner with Ron in hospitality than ever before.

On three other occasions, women newly released from the hospital and needing special care stayed with us until they were well enough to return to their own families. I was not a nurse by either skill or desire. God forced my servant's heart to expand.

Two other teens with problems at home lived with us, one for two years and another for six months. My chauffeuring duties seemed overwhelming at times. I learned to love other kids as if they were my own. I learned to make a lot out of a little at home—space, time, energy and food.

Young families moved in to try to get on top of their budgets before moving on. Families in transition stayed for several months. Single moms and their children became a part of our family.

Sometimes it was hard. Often I had to repent of self-pity and learn to address conflict rather than stuff resentment. I frequently read Matthew 25:34-36 to remind myself that Jesus evaluated the hospitality I extended to others as if he were receiving it himself. No other scripture had such power to change my selfish heart and motivate me to excellence. What a privilege to clean up after Jesus!

We have wonderful memories of those times! I am eternally grateful for what our hospitality contributed to the attitudes and character development of our children. We did make some mistakes, a few times making life too easy for people who should have been expecting more from themselves, but that was rare. In a quick tally, we remembered forty-two people who lived with us for at least a month, some for a year or more.

Hospitality now comes as naturally to me as it does to Ron. Sharing my home is one of the great joys of my life. There are items in our home that have no place in our lifestyle except for hospitality: an ever-full jar of homemade cookies (chocolate chip is my specialty), a big basket of toys, a high chair, a playpen, ample dishes and flatware, folding chairs, a sofa bed in Ron's office, children's videos, sleeping bags and extra pillows.

At last my heart embraces God's Word on the matter: I now offer hospitality without grumbling and with rejoicing.

Do nothing out of selfish ambition
or vain conceit, but in humility consider
others better than yourselves.

PHILIPPIANS 2:3

CHAPTER 14

Above All Things: Humility

SALLY HOOPER

Laughter filled the dining room as the guests excitedly awaited an exquisite Italian dinner. The aroma of oregano and basil filled the air. My good friends and wonderful husband of twenty-eight years were about to experience some delicious examples of my culinary talents, or so I thought—I excused myself and proceeded to the kitchen to bring forth my prized pasta. As I gently lifted the lid on the pot of boiling noodles, my heart skipped a beat. There in the center of the rapidly boiling water was a gigantic mass of pasta shaped like a ball! No matter how hard I tried, I could not separate the sticky mass. There was only one thing left to do...cry!

As my tears flowed, one of my guests, a very wise woman, came into the kitchen to help. She took a long look at the pasta ball, then an even longer look at me, hugged me so warmly and said, "Sally, in the other room is a group of friends around your table. What will impress them most about this evening and what they will remember is your hospitality, love and warmth. They will remember *how* you served, not *what* you served."

We decided to "slice" the ball of pasta, place a slice on each plate, and smother it with meat sauce. As an added precaution, we dimmed the lights for "atmosphere" as we presented each guest with an Italian feast!

Since that evening, I have had numerous dinners in my home. Some of these dinners have gone without a hitch, others have definitely not! But I have never forgotten the valuable lessons learned that night from the pasta ball experience. My goal since that time has been to make everyone who comes into the Hooper home feel special. Hospitality always includes the risk of being humbled. I am learning how much easier it is to handle the unexpected when I am humble to start with.

Offer What You Have with Gratitude

Our two oldest children, Dave, 27, and Leigh Anne, 24, were among the first disciples to plant churches in Russia. When we visited them in their homes, we were surprised by the lack of physical comforts they had, such as hot water, washing machines and abundant food. But their hearts were joyful as they shared what they had not only with us, but with many other disciples. It was very humbling to watch as their guests enthusiastically enjoyed their dinner consisting only of bread with a slice of tomato or cucumber. They were able to humbly offer what little they had.

During the time our family lived in Los Angeles, my husband and I led a group of disciples in Beverly Hills. Even though our house was 60 years old and small, the address carried the zip code of one of the glitziest cities in America (90210). I used to think, "What are we doing here?" This place was totally out of our league. Our furniture, dishes and clothing were practical and looked used. Our one car was not a BMW or a brand new Mercedes, but a six-year-old station wagon. Insecurity gripped me until I remembered that God wanted me to give these people a new heart, an unmaterialistic heart...his heart. We began having Bible talks and lots of parties in our home. Steve, our youngest and a high school sophomore at the time, began having his friends over. As they experienced the sense of family and genuine love in our home, they came more often. In fact, it was almost impossible to get them to leave.

We became known as the "party people" in our neighborhood. I even taught one of my L.A. friends how to fix southern-style chicken. I can vividly remember how she pulled up a stool right next to me in the kitchen to watch the process. Even though she was a very wealthy woman, she looked at me and said, "You have everything I would like to have." God taught me that people are hungry for the truth he brings to our lives and that only our pride keeps us from sharing what we have been given.

"In Humility Consider Others Better Than Yourselves"

Philippians 2:3 is one of my favorite scriptures, but it is one of the hardest to practice. Putting others first is the reason I want to be hospitable, but somehow my good intention can get caught up in, "I wonder what they will think of me? Is everything perfect?" I can often expend so much energy cooking and cleaning, that I am too exhausted to show my guests a good time! It is also a great temptation to apologize for unmatched place-settings or for dust on the coffee table. This makes our guests feel awkward and uncomfortable, while true hospitality makes others feel relaxed. Of course, I want to do my best to have my house neat and clean, but I do not want to lose focus on my guests if my house is not as I would wish it.

I have also learned that allowing my guests to follow me into the kitchen and chop tomatoes or set the table makes them feel more included and closer to me. It is a special bonding time I can have with them.

Hospitality also means an open home to out-of-town guests. We have been blessed so many times over the years by having disciples and friends live with us in our home for a night, many days or, in some cases, even weeks. This is the most humbling experience of all, because I cannot hide anything. They can see who I really am. They get to see what time I go to bed, what time I get up, and how I—and the house—look both times! They see how I treat my husband and children. And through these experiences, those who have spent the night in our home remain close to us forever.

Humility and Humor

We have to be humble to laugh at our mistakes. I remember a very special Thanksgiving day several years ago in Los Angeles. Kip and Elena McKean, Chris and Marty Fuqua and their families, along with our family were having dinner at our house. Elena, Chris, Leigh Anne and I were all in the kitchen preparing a spectacular feast. Leigh Anne's job was to take the turkey (twenty-two pounds) out of the roasting pan and place it on the serving platter. In the process, she dropped the pan, spilling all the juice and grease from the cooked turkey onto the kitchen floor. At first, silence filled the room as we all surveyed the damage. Then we broke out in peals of laughter as each one of us began "skating" across the floor on the towels in a massive clean-up effort!

It is very humbling for me to look back over the years and to realize that God has used Bill and me and our home to reach people for him and his kingdom. God has taught me that if we have people in our home, offering them whatever we have to share, we can much more easily help them to become part of his eternal family.

Let the peace of Christ rule
in your hearts, since as members of
one body you were called to peace.
And be thankful.

COLOSSIANS 3:15

Grateful for God's Blessings

MARCIA LAMB

"Thank you! This will be perfect. It's everything we need!" These words ricocheted off the walls of the tiny apartment and riveted deep into my heart. Ryan and Linda Howard were unloading the moving van that had just brought them to Chicago from a successful campus ministry in St. Louis. Roger and I had stayed in their home while our son, Michael, was at St. Louis Children's Hospital. I knew that this tiny cracker box of a place couldn't compare to the lovely home they had just left. When Ryan hung his favorite picture of an old man lovingly teaching a child to play the banjo, I knew that no matter where they lived, these two people knew how to create "home." Out of a heart of gratitude, Linda has created beauty and warmth in the most sterile, old, cold environments. As you get a glimpse of their home, you also get a glimpse of their hearts. The Howards are known for their gratitude to God and their hospitality. God has refined their hearts through many difficulties, and they have responded by offering their hearts and their home as a haven for many.

Ryan is now a professional counselor in San Diego. Linda is still a great example of one graciously living in a challenging situation. Her poor health and physical limitations set before her the daily challenge of being grateful for the not-so-perfect house in which her soul and spirit dwells. As I reflect on how she has always turned the least desirable surroundings into beautiful God-serving homes, I understand better how gratitude toward God is the highest motivation for our daily lives.

I must confess that I can remember many moments in my life when gratitude ricocheted *off* my heart. There was the night that my kitchen ceiling fell in and a waterfall gushed down my walls. But, I might have taken sweeping water out my kitchen door at 2:00 A.M. a little better if my new mother-in-law hadn't been spending the night for the first time!

A Time of Testing

Love is blind, but God still sees and exposes an ungrateful heart. Our first apartment was perfect, at least that is how we remembered it two months before we got married. The night we went to sign the lease, candles were glowing, beautiful paintings were hanging on the wall, soft music was playing in the background, and situated in the middle of everything was the bedroom. Imagine our shock when we arrived from our honeymoon to find that the paintings had covered fist-sized holes in the walls, the candles were nearly the only lights, the music drowned out the neighbors screaming next door, and yes, the bedroom was in the middle of everything! You couldn't go anywhere in that apartment without going through the bedroom. To add insult to injury, the shower had dripped all summer and left a moldy green aura in the bathroom, and the hot water heater had blown black soot everywhere.

God was giving me lesson number one in marriage: Be grateful! The look on poor Roger's face disclosed all the hopes of a gallant new groom about to be shattered. To be perfectly honest, I don't remember all that was said that day; I just remember cleaning and cleaning. But I must not have blown it too badly because my Prince Charming served me a dinner of soup and sandwiches—by candlelight, of course! I'm thankful I did not wound Roger that day with ingratitude for the way he was meeting my needs.

Later I came across a scripture that says so much about the importance of a wife having a grateful heart: "A wife of noble character is her husband's crown, but a disgraceful wife is like decay in his bones" (Proverbs 12:4). From what I understand, the pain of decaying bones is a deep unrelenting pain. The ungrateful spirit of a wife causes her husband pain that she may not immediately see, but that one day will destroy him. Next to her gratitude for God, a wife must reinforce her gratitude for her husband because that relationship is the foundation of the home.

People Over Things

False gratitude loves the gift more than the giver. Things become more important than people. Houses become showplaces instead of service stations. When I find myself on my knees washing dishes in the bathtub, when my trusty washer breaks down again, my favorite crystal wedding gift gets shattered, or a tornado, blizzard, earthquake or flood leaves my house in an altered state, I am reminded that I am capable of worshipping the created rather than the Creator. Have I run out in the yard and cursed God when these things have happened? Well, no, but I have lost my temper with my children, nagged my husband, worried over the bills, complained about the climate, and let "busyness" of home

Bring flowers, dessert or beverages and a thank-you note when invited to a meal at someone's house.

Bring a camera to a party, take pictures and surprise the host/hostess with photographs later.

Fax your feelings of love to keep in touch with distant churches and relationships.

Give "Levi dinners" (like in Luke 5:27-29) for friends and family of new converts to begin influencing them for God.

Bring or send special food items to friends in other countries, especially foods unavailable in their location. (For example, peanut butter, powdered milk, Jell-O, macaroni and cheese, etc., brought from the U.S. to Europe).

Choose "secret pals" by drawing names in discipleship groups. Bring homemade items or other gifts, plus encouraging anonymous notes each week to meetings. Reveal secret pal identities once per month.

Give children of evangelistic Bible study group members a piece of fruit to take home each week after the meeting to remind them of their purpose of helping Jesus and their parents produce "fruit" through the group's efforts.

Have each member of an evangelistic Bible study group bring a can of fruit or a piece of fruit to make a fruit salad. The leader provides the Jell-O pudding sauce, representing the love which combines the other ingredients. This demonstrates the need for unity in accomplishing the goal of the group.[*]

Each Sunday have a newer disciple over for a meal.

Bake special breads or cookies each week and deliver to non-Christians you are trying to impact with Jesus' love. These people may be coworkers, neighbors, parents of your children's classmates, etc.

[*]Recipe found in *The Fine Art of Hospitality Handbook* under "Fruit Salad," Theresa Ferguson.

Organize a clothing exchange (people bring clothes they no longer need and take clothes they can use) at the beginning of each season. This will be helpful to everyone who participates, especially to single moms. Invite non-Christians who might be in special need of such assistance.

Prepare fruit or food baskets to surprise those in need. Holiday seasons are especially good times for this type hospitality.

These and other similar acts of good will show that we care enough to give thought to the specific needs of others. Thoughtfulness shows a true love which unifies, encourages, provides memories and bonds hearts forever. Such demonstrations of love provide the proof that we are a part of the family of God! Let us develop the heart of Jesus by following Paul's admonition: "In everything I did, I showed you that by this kind of hard work we must help the weak, remembering the words the Lord Jesus himself said: 'It is more blessed to give than to receive'" (Acts 20:35). A truly thoughtful person will also be a thoughtful host or hostess.

Thoughtfulness When Having People
Over to Eat a Meal

- Ask earlier if they have food allergies or strong dislikes (or if they are vegetarian).

- If you are preparing a gourmet meal, have peanut butter and jelly on hand to offer to children.

- Think through seat placement instead of saying, "Just sit anywhere." Don't put all the quiet ones together and all the talkers together. Set your guests up for success.

- Offer both regular and decaf coffee for dessert. (Either have two coffeemakers or make one pot, pour into a carafe and then make another pot.)

- If you know that a guest is on a diet for weight control (or should be!), do not fix a rich, calorie-laden dessert. Offer something light and low-calorie.

- Think through ahead of time specific questions to ask your guests in order to get to know them better. Have funny stories from your own life ready to share if the conversation lags.

- Make mental (or written) notes about things your guests particularly like, and repeat those foods or features in the future. People feel special when you remember their likes and dislikes. (Example: Having Coffeemate on hand because a frequent visitor prefers it to milk.)

- Pray for God to inspire you with other ideas. You will be amazed at how thoughtful hospitality can become a daily part of your life with a little practice. And God promises, "A generous man will prosper; he who refreshes others will himself be refreshed" (Proverbs 11:25).

Take from our souls the strain and stress,
And let our ordered lives confess
The beauty of thy peace.

JOHN G. WHITTIER

CHAPTER 17

Peace That Passes Perfection

BETTY MOREHEAD

Far too often our experience with hospitality is "Children + Company + Cleaning = Chaos and Confusion." Bringing people into our homes to see who we really are, putting our family up for scrutiny as disciples and serving these guests can be stressful and scary unless God has built the house (Psalm 127:1) and directed our plans. Does being a host or hostess at peace seem like a contradiction in terms? Hebrews 12 says that peace is a by-product of discipline and training; in the same way, a peaceful attitude is the result of a struggle for righteousness.

What keeps us from being at peace is sin, but for me specifically, it is frequently unresolved conflict and unforgiveness which accumulate and then eat away at my relationships with others and God. The Bible calls this a bitter root (Hebrews 12:15) that defiles many. How can I tell if I have festering feelings? Recently I got irritated with my husband on what should have been a happy occasion—our son was home from college to be with the family for the day. Instead of being at peace, I was upset with how Stan had cooked the meat outside on the grill. Rather than stopping to consider why I was upset, I got critical of him, was disrespectful and then realized later that I needed to apologize. After he forgave me, I still felt unsettled. It took prayer and meditation on my motives to discover the root of the problem. I realized I was critical because I had been anxious about the events and the schedule of the day. In my arrogance I had worked out the way I thought the day should go, and when the events were different from my expectations, I was actually upset with God.

In this situation my festering feelings became obvious only *after* my reaction to the circumstances. For me some valid heart-test questions are (1) Am I controlled by the circumstances around me? and (2) When I have the need to serve, or to show hospitality, do I resent all the effort and personal sacrifice required to give to guests?

Showing Hospitality Brings Tests

Satan takes every opportunity to overwhelm us, but he especially uses the times during which we carry more responsibility. He wants us to feel overburdened and out of control. He sometimes gives us more than we can handle on our own (as he did Job).* That's the whole point: We were never designed to handle difficult things on our own. God's specialty is to step in and solve the impossible—if he is asked (2 Corinthians 1:9). After all, Satan cannot give us any test that God does not allow for our strengthening.

In Luke 17:1-6 Jesus speaks to the disciples about resolving conflict and forgiving those who hurt us. They realize just how challenging this is to practice and they beg for more faith. Jesus responds with two clues to implementing faith which relate to being a host or hostess with a peaceful heart. The first is the faith to expose the hurt in your own heart, giving the other person an opportunity to acknowledge that hurt and to repent. Then you need to beg God to take away the hurt feelings, whether or not they are acknowledged. The second is the faith to believe and *pray* for an unselfish attitude like the servant who meets the needs of others before his own.

If we resolve all our conflicts on a daily basis God's way, pray that he remove the bitterness, and then wrestle with God until he gives us an unselfish heart, hospitality will be a joy. The effect of this process in your heart is confidence and quietness in your attitude, and this impacts those around you. Isaiah sums it up:

> *The fruit of righteousness will be peace;*
> *the effect of righteousness will be quietness and*
> *confidence forever.*
> *My people will live in peaceful dwelling places,*
> *in secure homes,*
> *in undisturbed places of rest (Isaiah 32:17-18).*

Your home will be a haven for your family first, and then for all who visit you. Your guests will be drawn to your family and then to God because you reflect his nature. Restaurants offer atmosphere, excellent food, entertainment and relaxation. But, as disciples, we have a unique mission to give more to our guests: to give ourselves unselfishly as Jesus would. I can remember fixing and serving elaborate meals with the table set perfectly and each detail given careful attention, but realizing, at the end of the evening, that I had not participated in even one in-depth

---

*Revelation 2:10 tells us that Satan put some of the Christians into prison to test them even to the point of death. But God promises that each of us will not be tempted beyond that which we can bear (1 Corinthians 10:13).

conversation. My goal now is to offer my peaceful heart to my guests as Jesus did, not simply to give them an entertaining time devoid of stress and embellished with gourmet treats.

Planning Brings Peacefulness

In order for guests to feel relaxed, welcomed and happy when they are with us, we plan carefully. Stan and I pray that our preparations will lead us to meeting our guests' needs for fun, relationships and food. Some of the things we do to accomplish this are as follows:

Think carefully through the composition of the group so that our guests will enjoy each other and not just share a connection with us.

Consider which disciples to include for building relationships and for training in hospitality.

Plan the atmosphere most conducive to this (a video for the husband who is on the quiet side or a lively game for those who enjoy crowds and talking).

Eliminate as many interruptions as possible during dinner or a video.

Anticipate difficulties, such as rain for outdoor activities and tired young ones at Sunday lunch. (I keep a bag of toys handy and a clean bedroom for napping babies.)

Give attention to the basics: comfort of temperature, adequate lighting and cleared walkways during the snow and ice season.

Involve the guests as much as possible in the event, such as bringing food and helping to serve and cleanup.

Greet each person at the door upon arrival and walk them out at departure no matter what else is going on.

Our mentality should be "God loves each one of us, so how can I show that love to those who don't know God?" Jesus summed it all up when he said, "It is more blessed to give than to receive" (Acts 20:35). Serving will give us happiness if we're prepared to do it with an unselfish and forgiving heart. God will then give us a peaceful attitude, no matter what is happening around us.

CHAPTER 18

Are We Having Fun Yet?

EMILY BRINGARDNER

In every job that's to be done,
There is an element of fun;
Just find the fun, and snap! the job's a game.
And every task you undertake,
Becomes a piece of cake
A lark, a spree, it's very clear to see...*

Maybe it was clear for Mary Poppins to see, but for real people in real life, we too often find that we miss the fun altogether. Sometimes it is difficult to find the fun in some of our most basic tasks, responsibilities and privileges in life in the kingdom of God. Why? Because we aren't looking for it. We find what we look for—that's a promise from the Bible, you know! "Seek and you will find" (Matthew 7:7). When we find fun in our own lives, in our own households, then we can share it with those we invite into our homes.

Celebrating Life

When my sister, Sheila Jones, asked me to write this chapter, it struck me that fun had been a strong cord binding our hearts and lives together in our childhood years. I remember...as a child, making place cards for special dinners at our home...playing my guitar for big family gatherings...giving Dad a ball of string as a Christmas present. (He had to follow the string through the whole house to find that it was tied to his present: a red, overstuffed recliner.)...Mom wrapping a coin in aluminum foil and baking it in one of our birthday cakes. (Whoever got the coin in their piece would get a prize.)...family camping trips and vacations, sitting around a fire, looking at the stars and laughing together.

We are privileged that we can build families, both physical and spiritual. And both of these families need to be built on the special memories of fun. Fun makes life a celebration. Among other things, being hospitable means learning how to celebrate life with others. People need to see that disciples are

*"A Spoonful of Sugar," music and lyrics by Richard M. Sherman and Robert B. Sherman. *Mary Poppins* (Los Angeles: A Walt Disney Production) 1964.

free to have more fun than anyone (and they will wake up the next day and still feel good about it).

As a leader of college and single women, I had countless opportunities to have fun while being about my purpose of bearing fruit. When a new Christian received her Ph.D. in biophysics, we honored her with a dinner at my home (a singles' household). We borrowed beakers and test tubes from the chemistry lab, filled them with colored water, and combined them with candles for a centerpiece. We also gave her a lab coat to wear. To this day, all of us can remember the fun we had together. It was a wonderful time of celebration. Times like this build the special memories of living happily together in the family of God.

Fun Stealers

Several years ago, I realized that the fun was drying up not only in my hospitality, but in my life as well. Added ministry and home responsibilities had revealed my weaknesses in keeping a schedule and being slow to resolve conflicts. Jesus says, "The thief comes only to steal and kill and destroy" (John 10:10). We need to remember that it is Satan, the thief, who robs us of our fun. Of course, the thief shows up in many disguises. In my life, I did not humble myself and get help with scheduling. It was easier to be thoughtful and make people feel special and important when I didn't have to prepare meals on a regular basis or when I only had to bathe myself, not my children, to be ready for guests. I had to learn that with ever-increasing responsibility, there is a corresponding need for ever-increasing faith to help us maintain our friendships and outreach.

Other things that steal the fun, besides pride and poor planning, are unresolved family or household conflicts, self-pity and a self-focused concern about not having nice things. Sometimes we lose out on the fun because, like Martha in Luke 10, we are too worried about all that needs to be done and whether or not everything is "just right."

I'm grateful for the time I led the women in two churches in Southeast Asia. I was deeply touched by the simple hospitality of sisters who had so little to give materially but, like many women in the Bible, gave all they had. Once again, I was reminded that giving (hospitality) is an issue of the heart. I'm grateful that now, back in affluent southern California, I don't have to worry about having "all the right things" to entertain our friends. It is good to see that what really matters is giving my heart to the people God has given me to love. If I'm really giving my heart, it will be fun—whether I have a little or a lot.

Let People into Your Life

Consider a hospitality story in the Bible (Luke 15). There was a woman who found her lost coin and invited her friends in to rejoice with her—a reason for a party! Notice how much joy there is in sharing "happy endings." The more we allow people to know our risk and pain, the more they will be able to share our joy. Private people celebrate less.

I remember when we lived in Florida, and we had made the decision to sell our home and move to Boston. A woman called to come see the house. I was home with two small children, and things were not picture perfect, to say the least. I knew I could give up, or I could break my neck cleaning and probably lose my temper in the process. Or I could call a friend and get a plan. I remember that day...a couple of Christian friends came over, helped watch the kids, scrubbed my kitchen floor, and even taught me to put cloves and cinnamon on a cookie sheet in the oven so the house would smell like freshly baked cookies. We had a great time! We laughed a lot. And we all felt the joy when the sale went through. That day I shared my need with women I had studied the Bible with and had brought to the Lord. We must let people into our hearts, our lives, our kitchens if we are going to celebrate with them.

In Jesus' story of the prodigal son, the father said, "We had to celebrate and be glad" (Luke 15:32). That should be the heart and soul of every disciple. We should love celebrating with other people. My 10-year-old son's favorite movie of last year was *The Mask*. In it Jim Carrey as the Mask says, "P-A-R-T-Why? Because I gotta!" Life can be a celebration. We need to see that fun is vital to healthy, happy families and households. We are building special memories for both our physical and spiritual families. Let's allow God to use us in the lives of others so that they can celebrate life. That's how we need to feel about putting the fun in our hospitality. Why? "Because, we gotta!"

As Jesus and his disciples
were on their way, he came to a village
where a woman named Martha
opened her home to him.

LUKE 10:38

· Specific Life Situations ·

I have learned the secret of
being content in any and every situation,
whether well fed or hungry,
whether living in plenty or in want.

PHILIPPIANS 4:12

He tends his flock like a shepherd:
He gathers the lambs in his arms and
carries them close to his heart;
he gently leads those that have young.

ISAIAH 40:11

CHAPTER 19

Parents of Small Children

ROXANNE ARMES

"What?! Entertaining, when you have small children at home? Can this be done?" You may have asked these questions at one time or another. The answer is, "Yes, it can be done!" I actually experience this wonderful adventure at least once or twice a week.

Learning to Balance

I remember the first time I had dinner guests after my third child was born. My oldest daughter, Brittany, was five, Makhaila was two-and-a-half, and my newborn son, Bryce, was three weeks old. I started to work on dinner as I usually do, about an hour and a half before the guests were to arrive. As I was getting the food going on the stove, Bryce woke up crying loudly; he was starving. So, I ran and got him and fed him a little, put a pacifier in his mouth and went back to work. Then Brittany came in crying because she had hurt her elbow and needed Mommy to get her a Band-Aid. After that little emergency was over, I started to set the table and Makhaila came in and knocked over a glass and broke it. I had just finished cleaning that up when Bryce began to cry again because I had not fed him enough. So I sat down and fed him a little more, ran back into the kitchen just in time to find the potatoes boiling over on the stove. I thought, *That's it! Why did I ever try to do this?*

At that moment, I decided to pray! I asked God to send a few angels to watch over the kids and to help me get everything ready before my guests arrived. I wanted to be able to serve them and meet their needs. I went in and put a video on for Brittany and Makhaila, and Bryce went back to sleep. *Amen!* I did end up finishing everything in time, and I don't think the dinner guests even had a clue about how difficult that dinner was for me to prepare! You can face a lot of anxiety while preparing to entertain when you have small children because their needs are unpredictable. An emergency can arise at virtually any time! But, I have learned a few steps to cut down on the anxiety. Shortly after the above episode, I figured out how to work around Bryce's nursing schedule and how to get Brittany and Makhaila more involved in helping me to prepare. I learned that I needed to really think ahead and plan wisely. I have also realized that I should not choose something too time consuming or difficult to cook and that I should allow myself enough time for preparation.

I also discovered a few short cuts, such as finding quick and easy recipes. I prefer meals that can be whipped up in thirty minutes to an hour. I check to make sure I have everything I need and start preparing ahead of time. Sometimes I get things all ready to pop in the oven the night before. I even set the dining room table the night before if I know I will be short on time the next day.

Involve the Children

Getting the children involved is a key factor. If they are busy helping me prepare, they are less likely to get into trouble. When I am baking, my kids are usually sitting on the counter or standing on a chair watching. I let them add the ingredients or help stir. (They like to lick the bowl the best!) I really want my children to learn how to bake and then to share what they have baked with others. We bake all kinds of things at Christmas. I let them decorate the Christmas cookies while I work on some of the more difficult items. We give lots of goodies to our family and friends. We even used our wagon to deliver gift bags to our neighbors. The kids took turns handing them out and saying, "Merry Christmas!" Needless to say, they warmed many hearts!

I get my children involved in any way I can. They love to set the table, even if it is just folding napkins and placing the silverware. Sometimes I let them make the salad, or stir the lemonade, or watch the rolls so they can tell me when they are brown. It's very important for them to feel a part of serving. It definitely trains them from a very young age to be hospitable. If they are not involved, they can get bored and begin to demand my attention. If I don't include them, I begin to run around frantically and lose patience with them. If this happens in our homes, our kids will learn to resent having guests because it takes time away from them and turns Mom into "the wicked witch of the west"! (And then we wonder why they are not friendly when the guests arrive.)

Welcome!

Working together to prepare the house for the "Tour" is a great way to get them involved in cleaning up the house. Picking up their toys, taking things up to their rooms, and cleaning up their rooms are helpful jobs they can do. I tell them that we want the house to look extra warm and friendly and very clean for the Tour. Then when our guests arrive, the children love to be the tour guides. Usually they greet them at the door and after all the hugs and greetings, they say, "Do you want to see my room?" They take a lot of pride in showing off their rooms, especially if they have just cleaned them! Makhaila loves to show off the whole house, even the laundry room. This usually keeps everyone occupied just long enough for me to get the food on the table and be ready to seat them when they reappear.

Preparing our children to have hospitable hearts is very important. We all want our children to be warm and loving to guests; it's not always natural for them, so we must take the time and opportunities to teach them to be like Jesus. One of my children is very warm by nature and will easily give anyone a hug and make them feel special. The other two, however, from time to time need a little encouragement. We have found that if we prepare them ahead of time, they are ready and willing. We talk about who is coming over and how they can give of themselves to make the person or family happy. I tell them that Jesus needs us to be his arms. Since he is not physically here on this earth to hug everyone and to do nice things to make them feel special and encouraged, it is our job. We talk about how happy it makes God for us to do this.

If my children are not acquainted with the people coming over, I tell them what they look like, and I share something about their life to which the children can relate. For example, when I invited an older woman over for the first time, I told the children that our neighbor who lives right across the street from us was coming for dinner. I told them that she is a grandma and that they could call her Grandma Kay. I also told them that Grandma Kay needed lots of hugs just like their grandmas do. We talked about how they could make her feel special and loved by being really nice, giving warm hugs, singing a song for her and telling her about their day. They colored pictures for her too, which helped them feel prepared for her visit. When she arrived they were very happy to hug her and give to her.

Even if our guest is a relative or someone that the children know well but have not seen for a while, we still prepare them. We might say, "What are you going to give Nana and Papa when they get here?" They respond, "Hugs and kisses!" Then they usually go off and make a gift or color a picture to give to them.

If one of the children is not having a good day or is in a bad mood, we try to deal with it before our guest arrives. Then, hopefully, we will have avoided an uncomfortable scene. This sets our children up for success. Their hearts and minds are in gear, and they are ready to give of themselves.

Learning to Share

Sharing their toys or their room is something that challenges most children. Have you ever heard a mother say, "I don't know what is wrong, he never fights over toys at other people's houses, just when we are at home"? Children often get protective and selfish when it comes to their own toys and their own rooms. Have you heard them say, "Well, this is my room" or "This is my toy"? It is important to have people into your home often so that your children get accustomed to sharing their possessions. This is another area that it is good to talk about ahead of time. Explain that there are children coming over and that it's going to be a lot of fun sharing their toys. Or, "Tonight you can let our guest use your bed. Let's make a welcome sign and leave it on the pillow. Then they will feel right at home."

We teach our children that God gave us everything we have to share with others. The guest can choose which video he wants us to watch. If there is an argument over a toy, we must offer it to our guest. (After all, we live here, and we get to play with that toy or watch that video anytime we like!)

Whether you have one small child or several, being hospitable can be a real challenge. Remember, the most important part of hospitality is not the food, but the friendship. Children and hospitality are both blessings from God. The two can go hand-in-hand instead of working against each other. Children can warm even the hardest heart and be a shining example of God's love. Jesus said it as well as it can ever be said: "I tell you the truth, unless you change and become like little children, you will never enter the kingdom of heaven" (Matthew 18:3).

CHAPTER 20

Working 9 to 5

SHEILA JONES

"What is the most difficult challenge you face as a result of working outside the home?" This is a question I recently asked a group of about twenty working women, mostly married. The overwhelming majority responded not with a specific problem at work, but with the frustration of meeting their family's needs while being responsible at their jobs. They did not feel good about the way they were keeping their homes—cleaning and washing and cooking. Most of all, they wanted to better meet the emotional and spiritual needs of their children and their husbands.

When we feel torn and guilty all the time, we are not much good to anybody. Our limited energy reserves leak out of guilt-ridden holes, rendering us even less able to meet the emotional and spiritual needs surrounding us. To think of offering hospitality to people on a consistent basis becomes overwhelming when we are feeling exhausted, frustrated and guilty. How can we plug up those holes and focus our energy in positive, faithful ways?

Jesus gives a clear answer, as he always does: "Seek first his kingdom and his righteousness" (Matthew 6:33). The truth of Jesus' statement is reflected in Dr. Seuss's story about Bartholomew Cubbins and his many hats. Each time he removed one hat to show respect for the king, another one sat on his head. After removing 499 hats, he finally got to the bottom of it all—a magnificent, jewel-studded, purple-plumed hat of all hats.

As working women, we must wear many hats. In fact, I asked a group of working women to take two minutes to write down some of the hats they wear. One woman, gifted with a quick-thinking cap, wrote down twenty-five! But the point is, no matter how many hats we wear (including the hat of the hospitable hostess), we will not wear them well unless we wear the hat of all hats underneath them—the hat of seeking first to please God. We cannot balance the 499 without first carefully placing on our heads the foundational one.

Prayer and Planning

Much has already been said about the need to plan. The working woman, especially one who is married with children, simply will not be able to function well in all her different roles if she does not take time every week to plan. But even weekly planning will not enable us to wear all the hats...only prayer will bring the peace and steadiness to maintain our spiritual lives day in and day out. And if there is anything the working woman needs, it is a sense of peace in her fast-paced life.

For years I posted a weekly menu on the refrigerator. My middle daughter was the type who always planned ahead, even when she was a child. When I would finally get all three girls in bed and was almost ready to pass out in a state of exhaustion myself, Bethany would look at me and ask the inevitable question, "What are we having for breakfast?" I would maintain my composure, take a deep breath and say, "I don't know." It was to the advantage of my mental health at that point to have a menu posted so she could know what was happening the next morning. Naturally speaking, I never gave too much thought to the next day in my life. I totally experienced today and gave it my all, but tomorrow hardly ever entered my mind.

It seems that people are either *born planners* or *born let-it-happeners*; I naturally am a let-it-happener. But through the years I have had to learn to think ahead, to plan, to be organized. Since I started working a 9-to-5 job four days a week, I have had to learn even more. Somewhere along the way I had stopped posting my menu. I don't think it was just because Bethany stopped asking and went off to college. I think I got too busy and my life was running me, rather than the other way around. I sometimes did a menu and sometimes didn't. When I didn't do one, I hated that feeling that came over me at four o'clock in the afternoon when I thought, *What are we going to have for supper?*

I spent some effort (and time) reevaluating my priorities and goals. More than ever I am learning to plan ahead and budget my time according to the most important needs.

These days I sit down at a specific time to plan and pray through all the different aspects of my week, to set specific goals in different relationships and areas of responsibility. During this time, I make up my weekly menu, and to the side, I make an accompanying list of all the ingredients needed to produce each meal (even down to eggs and milk). Then I make a grocery list of needed items, and make notes throughout my daily planner reminding me what I need to do to prepare ahead of time for the next day's meal, e.g. "Snap beans while talking to Jack and

Barb on Tuesday night." I make promises to myself and evaluate at the end of the week how I've done in following through with those promises, e.g. "Get up as soon as the alarm goes off."

In order to have people over and feel good about it, I must have a sense of organization in my home and in my life. Although I tend to think I work well under pressure, I am sure that I work better, calmer and more joyfully when I plan ahead.

Ask Others to Help

Children. I came from a home where my mother graciously fixed many meals for people all by herself. I'm ashamed to say that my sister and I did not help very much during those times. Mother should have expected more of us, to be sure, but I have seen the pattern repeat itself. When we have had company over through the years, I have tended to get meals ready and serve them all by myself, too. If I had it to do over, I would expect more out of my girls during their younger years. Since I did not work outside the home then, I *could* do it all, and I did. But to the extent that we do this, we rob our children of an understanding of their responsibilities in serving.

Friends. We also need to ask for help from others more often. When we invite people for dinner and they ask to bring something, we usually should let them. When I fix the meal, but someone else brings a tossed salad, I am so encouraged to see it arrive. They are happy because their contribution was not time consuming, but they are about to enjoy a full meal with friends.

My prideful tendency is not to ask people to do something because it may not be done the way I want it done. Instead of taking the time to explain how I would like it, I just do it myself. When time and energy are limited, as they both are for me at this point in my life, I need to explain, assign and trust others to do it excellently.

Working has caused me to have to rely on others more. Several mornings ago I left an egg boiling on the stove. I realized this when I was already at work (thirty minutes away). I was on my way back home to turn it off, thus wasting an hour of prime work time, when my husband asked, "Isn't there someone you could call to go in the basement door and turn it off?" The truth was that the seldom-used entrance had cobwebs and the storage area and hallway were in a mess. My pride hated for anyone to see that area of my house (and my life!). I died to my pride and called a friend to go over, and to this day she *still* loves and respects me!

Groups. Our house is used often for group activities both during the week and the weekend. I have talked with the "regulars" about their responsibility to help with clean up. Instead of getting attitudes, I got honest and told them that when we as a group use any home, we as individuals are responsible for cleaning and straightening it afterwards. Most people are willing to help; they simply have not been taught or shown what to do. But in order to have help, we must be willing to have other people opening our refrigerators and cabinets and drawers. The more we keep order in our homes, the easier it is for others to help us put things away.

Working women leave for work early the morning after an evening activity and cannot afford to say, "Don't worry. Just leave it. I'll get it later." But I'm afraid that sometimes people say just that, and then inform someone several weeks later, "It's just too hard on me to have group meetings in my home. Someone else will have to do it for a while." Since hospitality certainly includes offering our homes for group activities, we must learn to communicate to others how they can help us be able to do it.

"Another Saturday Night"

For working women, perhaps the best night to invite people for dinner is Saturday (or whichever day they have off). But it is tempting to be selfish with our day off since it is our only day to do this and that and everything else. Good planning is needed because if we put everything off until Saturday, we will usually be frustrated and even tense on that all-important day. If we do a few well-planned errands during the week, we will not be so overwhelmed on Saturday.

But busy day or not, we can still have people over. We simply need to plan carefully and put something on to cook while we are doing other jobs in the house or yard. If several weekends have passed and we have not even thought about inviting friends, either disciples or nondisciples, to have dinner or coffee and dessert, then we are letting our busy lives run us and squeeze out the time to practice hospitality. The truth is, we need it as much as the people we invite!

As disciples, we must decide that it is God's will for us to open our homes to others, to share our food with others, to take time and energy to serve others. If we are not doing this and are excusing our lack of hospitality by saying, "I'm just too busy," we need to reevaluate, repent and resolve to get the help we need. We must learn all over again that to serve others is to be truly refreshed ourselves.

Housekeeping and Hospitality Tips
for the Working Woman

• Decide what jobs need to be done and how often, whether daily, twice a week, weekly, twice a month, monthly, semiannually or annually. Work out a plan to get these jobs done.

• When you have a plan, you can take advantage of small amounts of time to do small jobs (such as scouring the sink). When you don't have a plan, you might wander the house for five minutes and get discouraged at the work you don't have time to do.

• If you can afford it, hire some help from time to time to do cleaning or ask a friend for help.

• Buy meat in large quantities and store in the freezer; keep a supply of food you use often.

• Fix some or all of a meal in the morning before you leave for work. It is encouraging to come home to an already-prepared meal.

• Have on hand the ingredients for a meal that can be fixed quickly if unexpected guests arrive. (For example, fry and drain hamburger meat, and add it to prepared spaghetti sauce. It seems much more homemade and is ready very quickly.)

• If you have a kitchen at work, some food can be prepared during your lunch break (if the kitchen is not too full of people and if your boss doesn't mind).

• Have theme dinners and assign each person a dish or item to bring.

• Make double portions of casseroles and freeze one for later.

May the God of hope fill you with
all joy and peace as you trust in him, so that
you may overflow with hope by the
power of the Holy Spirit.

ROMANS 15:13

CHAPTER 21

Single Parent

Widowed
JOYCE CONN

Divorced
BARBARA MANUPUTY

Widowed: No Retiring From Hospitality

As the wife of Calvin, an evangelist and later an elder, I experienced hospitality in many forms. I was in opulent homes where servants dressed in uniform satisfied our every whim, and I was in homes where I knew the whole weekly food budget was spent on the meal prepared for my family.

I always felt honored and encouraged when disciples invited us into their homes, but the occasion most vivid in my memory was a couple of hours in the home of Mariann Maxwell. Thirty years have passed, but the memory of Mariann still disciples me.

Calvin had been invited to speak to a church in Indiana every evening for a week. As was the custom, families in the church invited us to dinner. One evening we went to Mariann's home. She apologized for the clutter since they were moving across the country in two days. Her husband had already left; she and her young son were finishing the packing. The curtains were off the windows, and boxes were all around the wall, but in the center of her dining room was a small card table set for four. She had bought fresh flowers for the centerpiece. The dinner was simple but well prepared. Mariann and her son were genuinely happy to have us in their home. I was so touched by her heart that I was determined never to forget her, but I didn't realize at the time how much I would need the lesson she taught me.

Throughout the years, people often stayed with us. Those who were going into the ministry might stay for a few months. Others who were going through particularly difficult times, such as a sister who had been threatened with physical harm, also stayed with us. There was nothing my husband enjoyed more than finding people in the Sunday morning fellowship who needed the encouragement of a home-cooked meal and time with family. I spent most Saturday evenings in the kitchen preparing huge casseroles, desserts and homemade rolls; I never knew how many would be coming to dinner. Our Sunday meal was so much fun with everyone sitting around our large table laughing, talking and sharing stories.

Taking It Deeper

After twenty-eight years of marriage, Calvin died of cancer. Joseph, our youngest son, and I moved to New Jersey while my two older sons stayed with friends in South Carolina so they could finish school. As I tried to rethink my role in the church as a single parent, my mind went back to Mariann and her son. I realized two things: (1) The church still needed for me to give my heart and home to others. There will always be that need. Dad was gone, but we were still a family, and as a family we would share our home. (2) Joseph, who was then six, needed to be in the company of strong Christian men often. He still needed to be with other families.

Now when we invite couples over, Joseph is the man of the house and serves well in that role. He never runs out of things to show our guests, or stories and jokes to tell. Then there's always basketball or ping pong.

We enjoy having single moms over with other couples. We like to mix it up. I know God is pleased when we play an active part in helping disciples get to know one another or in helping a young boy without a father become friends with a great role model. In all this, Joseph is learning to share and serve. That is what the disciple's life is all about.

Keeping On

It would be so easy, after many years of serving a husband, rearing children and constantly sharing our home, to feel like stepping back and relegating this role to younger women. Last Christmas morning, as always, I got up before everyone else and went downstairs to start preparing a Christmas feast. As I pulled the defrosted turkey out of the refrigerator and plopped it on the counter top, I stood there thinking, *How many of these "birds" have I stuffed? Forty, probably fifty.* At that moment I was strongly tempted to retire my recipes. I thought, *It would be so easy next year to make a casserole to take to someone else's home. I would like to read to the children or work a jigsaw puzzle while someone else takes care of the last minute details. I would like to ask, "Isn't there anything I can do?" and be answered with, "No, just relax."*

Then I thought of the people coming to my house that day: good friends and those who needed someone to share Christmas with them. I would never want my house to be empty on Christmas Day. I will always want people sitting around the same large dining room table sharing my home, my food, my life. I realized there is no place for a retired hospitality-giver in the kingdom. The needs are too many. I'm sure God feels as strongly about retired talents as he does about buried ones. Paul's words in Galatians call me higher:

> *Let us not become weary in doing good, for at the proper time we will reap a harvest if we do not give up. Therefore, as we have opportunity, let us do good to all people, especially to those who belong to the family of believers (Galatians 6:9-10).*

I'm grateful God has given me this role of service. I'm grateful for Mariann Maxwell. I've lost touch with her, but if she, too, is a widow, I pray the church is honoring her as she deserves (1 Timothy 5:10). Amid boxes and bare walls, she spoke volumes about the fine art of hospitality.

Divorced: In Giving We Receive

Nothing in my ten years as a disciple prepared me for divorce. At the age of eighteen, I had married my childhood sweetheart. Both of us had been reared in very religious homes, and both of us believed our marriage would last a lifetime. After studying the Bible, we became true disciples. We learned to love God wholeheartedly and to love both those inside and outside the church.

Our home became an instrument of hospitality. We imitated the lives of Ron and Linda Brumley, two disciples who have perfected the fine art of inviting others into their home and into their hearts, and we patterned our lives after theirs. It was not uncommon for us to have thirty to forty people over for lunch after Sunday service, or to bring home all of the stray singles after an evening service and fill them with homemade sourdough pancakes and sausage washed down with gallons of orange juice. Many in the kingdom felt our home was theirs, and many outside God's family would comment on the warmth they felt while in our home. Along with our two daughters, we experienced many happy times.

The Divorce

But the day came when the unthinkable became a heartrending reality: my husband left God and left our family. As his heart had grown cold toward God, his desire to have others into our home had begun to die as well; and before he left, having other Christians over had become a rare event.

The loneliness I felt after he left seemed unbearable. I remember wanting the comfort of my spiritual family around me. The very next weekend I invited some divorced and widowed sisters over for a cook-out. A sister came and stayed with me for a couple of weeks, bringing her hospitality into my home to serve me during a time of intense need. A house that had grown cold from a lack of love and hospitality was beginning to come to life again, even in the midst of pain. God was teaching me that healing comes through giving yourself away.

The Move

Six months later my youngest daughter, Amanda, and I moved to Boston. For the first seven months, we lived with other families. I was truly a displaced homemaker. The old familiar things I had used to serve others during my twenty-three years of marriage were no longer there, but thank God I was with people who practiced hospitality and allowed me the freedom to use their homes and their possessions to do the same.

Two years after moving to Boston, God blessed my daughter and me with a home of our own. What a joy it is to be able to use it to serve others. Thanksgiving has become a time to invite into our home those who have no place to spend the holiday. We have had as many as fifteen guests overnight in our two-bedroom condo, twenty-two for sit-down dinner, forty-five for dessert. It's been great to offer our home to a married couple for a weekend getaway while we *gotaway* somewhere else.

In Giving We Receive

In Acts 20:35 Luke quotes Jesus as saying, "It is more blessed to give than to receive." And, indeed, God's truth has borne fruit in my life. In giving away my home and my heart to others, God has provided, through my brothers and sisters in Christ, family for my broken family, fathers and sisters and brothers for my children and grandchild. And he has given me the husband for whom I have always longed and prayed. This past May, I married my best friend, Jack, (who, by the way, was the recipient of a good deal of my hospitality!). I praise God that I get to be a wife again and that together we can fulfill his command to "practice hospitality" (Romans 12:13).

I'm grateful, too, that I did not wait until I had a home of my own, or until I had a husband, or until everything was just right in my life to extend myself to others; for it is in giving that we receive; it is in giving that we are most like Jesus; it is in giving that our needs are truly met and we are truly fulfilled. God cannot bless us unless we are willing to focus our eyes on others.

Jesus is in heaven now preparing to share his heavenly home forever with us. How can we dare expect to enjoy his hospitality if we are not sharing our homes here on earth? If the love of God fills our hearts, it will fill our homes as well. We must let it spill over into the streets of our neighborhoods, to our friends, to our family outside of the kingdom, and even to strangers.

If you are a single parent, never let that keep you from showing hospitality. Don't hold back your heart or your home; share them now; share them tomorrow; share them forever. And God will bless you beyond measure.

I can do everything through him
who gives me strength.

PHILIPPIANS 4:13

CHAPTER 22

Physically Challenged

Self
MARCIA LAMB

Spouse
DIANE BROWN

Self: She Got Up to Serve

In the lonely moments before I was taken to surgery to remove a deadly uterine cancer, thoughts, revealing thoughts, flooded my mind. These are the thoughts I pushed aside to be brave for my family or to be brave for myself. But the thoughts rushed through the barriers of pretension and demanded my attention. Fears, doubts, self-pity. I am well-acquainted with these. I have faced them many times before, so I pulled out my arsenal of scriptures to combat them (Psalms 139, 136; Proverbs 2:5-8). However, I let one thought slip past my shield of faith…"You will be served." I liked that thought, so I lingered on it for a while. As the anesthetic began to take its effect physically, my soul was being anesthetized by the thought of all the attention I would surely be receiving.

Not the Way I Pictured It

After the blur of the first few weeks passed, the phone calls, the flowers, visits and meals dropped off. That is to be expected, but the unexpected also happened. Suddenly, all the people I was closest to were not available. My husband, Roger, was called out of town to deal with an urgent matter. My mother-in-law had to fly to the side of a dying relative. The ministry was at a crisis point that demanded key people to move from city to city to resolve the potential problems. Everyone seemed to be going through a personal crisis. My caring parents then came to help. They cleaned and cleaned, as if a sterile environment would ensure my recovery. But their own feelings of helplessness to cure me gave way to frustration. By this time, I was nearly devastated. "Hello, God! Where are you? Hey, this doesn't feel like love."

Becoming Like Jesus

As usual, the answer was at the cross. I pondered Jesus' experience in the Garden, a time when he too felt very alone in his anguish. Where were his friends? Why weren't they there to comfort him? Luke 22:45 says that he found his disciples asleep, "exhausted from sorrow." Their own personal sorrow had drained their strength so that they could not see or meet Jesus' greater need. But God was there. Jesus, after he had been strengthened by God, got up to serve our eternal need by giving his whole life. Had I let my personal sorrow miss the greater need of Christ? I had. Did Jesus let his greater need keep him from serving us? He didn't.

God always gives us living examples of people who have learned to be like him in different areas so that we will not be tempted to think, *Only Jesus could do that, and I'm not Jesus.* Mark 1:29-31 tells of Jesus healing Peter's mother-in-law. As soon as the "fever left her...she began to wait on them." I have a mother-in-law like that. Irene has suffered two strokes over the past year, and though her pace has slowed a bit, her heart is still very hospitable. Few days go by that she and her husband do not have people in their home. She has helped at least two women become disciples in her "weakened" state.

Another "warrior" of hospitality is Lena Geiling. Lena and Wayne served the church in Charleston, Illinois, in the shepherding role for many years. They kept Roger and me, Kip and Elena McKean, and John and Nancy Mannel encouraged as they opened their home to us time and again. They played a vital role as spiritual grandparents for our young student disciples at critical points in their lives. In spite of a serious stroke that left her paralyzed on her right side, Lena amazed us by her enduring spirit of love and hospitality. Just like the widow in Luke 21:1-4 who gave all that she had, Lena coped with her handicap with the help of her husband and his inventions. A cutting board with nails protruding held lettuce, roasts and her famous homemade breads while she sliced away "with one hand tied behind her back."

Low Energy: Deep Love

To our joy and to the glory of God, after five years I was declared cancer-free. But because of other health concerns (including hypoglycemia and fibromyalgia), I have a very low energy level. I have learned to manage my energy so that I can give my best strength where it is needed the most. I have to give my energy to housecleaning at the time of the day when I am physically strongest. Some days my energy must go to more mental tasks such as writing. Many days I need to nap so I can give my best to my family or to someone with whom I am studying the Bible in the evening. I learned to quit getting angry at my body, to forgive it for not being all I had hoped for, and to take care of it so that it can be used to God's glory (1 Corinthians 6:19). Letting faith rule in all circumstances is the key (Isaiah 40:28-31).

Planning is important to those of us with physical challenges. I have tried to be prepared for hospitality by keeping my coffee pot handy and my shelves stocked. My mother-in-law frequently cooks double portions and freezes some for later. Then she is always prepared to take emergency meals to the sick or to serve herself and her husband on those "bad-body days." I've learned from her to carefully plan my storage space, which saves me a lot of wasted energy. I keep supplies for cleaning, cooking or office work in the immediate area in which I use them. If you have physical limitations, you can still get your heart prepared to make people feel loved and welcome by planning ahead.

Let people serve you. Too many times our pride keeps us from accepting help. Besides being a sin, pride keeps us lonely and isolated. Invite the meal provider to stay and share the meal they have cooked. Spend a few moments giving to the people who have come to help you and freely express your gratitude.

See That Someone Meets the Need

While dealing with my own physical challenges, I have also observed the hospitable hearts of bedridden leaders. God has used many women, such as Elena McKean, Lisa Johnson and Joyce Arthur, even during difficult pregnancies, to be the motivators and initiators for serving others in need. I think of women like Erica Kim and Donna Lamb who, in spite of their own serious illnesses, have served the needs of thousands of women. They have shown me that if I cannot personally meet the need, I can still have the heart to see that someone does.

When God, through Jesus' human limitations, had accomplished all that he could do, he sent the Holy Spirit to work in and through disciples. When we reach our own physical limits, let's remember we can always "send the Spirit" by encouraging others to serve.

Spouse: A New Understanding of Hospitality

On the third day of my husband's hospitalization, he had become totally paralyzed on his left side with what would be diagnosed later as
Multiple Sclerosis. I remember with crystal clarity the doctor taking me
aside and saying, "You'll need to cancel your trip to L.A. this weekend.
You'll need to cancel any plans you have to travel in the foreseeable
future. We're dealing with something serious here. You'll need to get
ready to deal with a few changes in your life."

Doctors are given to understatement.

A Different Kind of Culture Shock

I knew what culture shock felt like. We'd lived for eight years in
Argentina and for brief periods in Guatemala and Mexico. That's like
jerking the rug of all life's social cues out from under you. This was a
very similar, familiar feeling. From the moment the ambulance came to
carry Steve to the hospital, everything about life was unplowed terri-
tory. You would think that the major adjustments would have to be made
by Steve. But we discovered that this was something that had happened
to the whole family; we would all have to adjust

Thank God Steve regained minimal use of his left side, but the fa-
tigue brought on by the MS also severely limited his activities. So much
of our everyday lives was radically changed. Now I was everybody's chauf-
feur, instead of splitting the driving with my husband. (No small order
with three teenage kids and a preschooler!) I had sole possession of the
checkbook(!)—and the bills—and the bank statement. (It's true that what
you most fear will eventually find you!) Chores that were commonly
shared suddenly became my responsibility. Our daily routine had to be
reordered to fit Steve's maximum energy hours. There were these and
many, many more adjustments to make, not the least of which was chang-
ing our attitude toward service—and as part of this, our attitude toward
hospitality. As leaders in the Dallas church, having people in our home
was a vital part of our ministry. I was personally affected as God used
Steve's MS to take me out of my comfort zone and to challenge my
selfishness.

In the course of time, I began to be tempted with thoughts like,
"Someone else just needs to carry the load of offering hospitality. I'm
hurting so much myself, how can I be expected to use my home to serve
people at a time like this?" Our kids developed the same attitude, of
course. (They always end up imitating what they see. I hate it when that
happens!) They had to take up the slack in the chores around the house,

learn to be responsible and, in general, grow up. But since I wasn't rising to the challenge, neither were they. The thought of having people in our home was a tension-filled, burdensome proposition.

At that time we wanted to spend some time with Todd and Tanya Spath who were new leaders in the church. Their small apartment couldn't accommodate our large family, so they had the audacity to just invite themselves over. In the state that my heart was in, you can imagine all the under-the-breath phrases I was mumbling. But an incredible thing happened! The whole family pitched in to pull off a very enjoyable evening, and miraculously, a new spirit came into our household. I feel really indebted to Todd and Tanya for insisting on that evening together. Giving had begun to heal us.

Healing Through Hospitality

It is very appropriate that in Webster's dictionary, the definition for "hospitable" is wedged between the word "hospice," which is a shelter, and the word "hospital," which is a place of healing. God says as much in Isaiah 58:6-8:

> *"Is not this the kind of fasting I have chosen:*
> *to loose the chains of injustice*
> *and untie the cords of the yoke,*
> *to set the oppressed free*
> *and break every yoke?*
> *Is it not to share your food with the hungry*
> *and to provide the poor wanderer with shelter—*
> *when you see the naked, to clothe him,*
> *and not to turn away from your own flesh and blood?*
> *Then your light will break forth like the dawn,*
> *and your healing will quickly appear;*
> *then your righteousness will go before you,*
> *and the glory of the LORD will be your rear guard."*

Truly, healing came as we gave to others. Since that historic dinner, God has used those ugly, sinful days to show me a lot about myself and about the nature of hospitality.

Hospitality before pride. Before, hospitality meant going to incredible lengths to be the "perfect hostess." The new adjustments in my life meant that I just had to ignore a few dustballs and relax a little. As I relaxed, I found that my guests relaxed too. People began to feel comfortable propping their feet on my coffee table, and I didn't mind! Some have even been known to fall asleep on the couch! This new perspective on hospitality frees up my time so that I'm not a slave to preparation for guests. As another side benefit, I could also feel great about allowing guests to vacuum or sweep the kitchen floor. This new attitude allows me to write this article as I prepare for a couple to come over for dinner without freaking out. In other words, being hospitable, as God commands, has helped me deal with the pride in my heart at a deeper level. As I lay aside my pretenses, the people we have in our home can lay theirs aside as well.

Accepting the limitations. After I got out of my pity party, I had to deal with a new set of facts in our lives. Part of Steve's illness is that he is constantly fatigued. He must rest for a considerable length of time daily. This surfaced a new mind game for Satan to play with me. When I don't open my home, am I just being selfish and a wimp, or is this really a time to protect my family and Steve? Thank God we're in the kingdom of God where, in most cases, someone has had similar experiences and can offer spiritual perspective. I have become more convinced than ever about the need for opening up my life to others whom I love and trust. I don't want to succumb to the temptation to have an "I'm the only one who's ever been through this, so you can't possibly hope to understand" attitude.

Hospitality for this physically-challenged family has meant learning about service. It's meant learning to take our eyes off our own challenging set of circumstances, reaching down deep inside our hearts and giving to others. In doing so, we have found that the ones we serve have not received the biggest blessing...we have!

Love One Another

After reading *The Fine Art of Hospitality*, hopefully you feel convicted and encouraged, but you may also feel a bit overwhelmed. Probably more than ever you realize the importance of having a heart of hospitality. To be sure, we should all be sobered as we hear Jesus' words which were quoted in the introduction:

> *Then the king will say to those on his right, "Come, you who are blessed by my Father; take your inheritance, the kingdom prepared for you since the creation of the world. For I was hungry and you gave me something to eat, I was thirsty and you gave me something to drink, I was a stranger and you invited me in, I needed clothes and you clothed me, I was sick and you looked after me, I was in prison and you came to visit me" (Matthew 25:34-36).*

Certainly Matthew 25 speaks of a salvation issue; we are to have a kind and hospitable heart toward others. And the Scripture does specifically command us to "practice hospitality" (Romans 12:13). In keeping perspective, though, we must realize that being perfect in our planning and execution of a party or dinner is *not* a matter of salvation. Having dust on a coffee table for two weeks will not cause the gates of heaven to close in our faces. I seriously doubt that we will stand before God and hear him say, "You really had a heart for people and meeting their needs while you were on the earth, but do you remember when you lived on Sieger Street and you invited your next door neighbors over for dinner? Well, the roast was a bit dry, and you had the fork on the wrong side of the plate. And that time that you hosted a shower for the new mom and used blue decorations when she had just had a seven-pound baby girl.... Also, I know you loved your family and gave of yourself to meet their needs, but your dust-bunny tally under your furniture came in at an all-time high."

Get my point? Balance is always the key, isn't it? Some go to one end of the spectrum (being rigid, fastidious, perfectionist) while others tend toward the other end (being disorganized, spacey, even lazy). This book is designed to help us take seriously our responsibility to show hospitality, but on the other hand not to take ourselves too seriously. Our works, no matter how well performed, cannot save us. Only the blood and grace of Jesus can do that. God's admonitions and commands always speak to the heart of an issue, and the heart of hospitality is simply loving other people. Jesus' new command to love each other was also an old command—one given new meaning by Jesus' life and sacrifice.

Should we plan ahead and do things to make others feel special? Yes! Should we realize the importance of keeping our homes ordered to reflect the nature of God? Yes! Should we seek to meet the needs of others in an unselfish, fun-filled manner? Yes again! As disciples, we should be seeking excellence and making progress in all areas, including that of hospitality. In doing our best to grow in our practice of hospitality, though, we must always remember that loving people is more important that impressing them.

This book was written to help us evaluate our hearts toward hospitality and to motivate us to change where needed—with the help of God. It was written to help us express and reflect the nature of God to others, to practice a godly art with a godly heart. Let's commit ourselves to enjoy the privilege of combining food, fellowship, fun and fruit-bearing to the glory of God. Let's be restorers of this fine art of hospitality.

Contributors

Roxanne Armes Washington, D.C.
Gloria Baird Los Angeles
Emily Bringardner Los Angeles
Diane Brown Dallas
Linda Brumley Chicago
Ron Brumley Chicago
Joyce Conn New York
Betty Dyson Boston
Theresa Ferguson Boston
Sally Hooper Dallas
Sheila Jones Boston
Geri Laing Triangle, N.C.
Marcia Lamb Los Angeles
Barbara Manuputy Boston
Kay McKean Boston
Greg Metten Los Angeles
Shelley Metten Los Angeles
Betty Morehead Boston
Thomas and Gillian Nolte Dusseldorf, Germany
Inga Ostrander Boston
Jeanie Shaw Boston
Kim Strondak Nashua, N.H.
Helen Wooten Los Angeles

About the Editor

Sheila Presley Jones holds certification for teaching secondary English and serves as women's editor of Discipleship Publications International. She and her husband Tom, who serves as managing editor for DPI, have lived in the Boston area for eight years. They have three daughters, ages 16, 19 and 23 years. Over the last 26 years, she and her husband have worked with churches in four states, leading evangelistic efforts and numerous workshops on marriage, family and spiritual growth. She has coedited two books on women of the Bible and a series of devotional books on various topics.

· Personal Inventory ·

Search me, O God,
and know my heart; test me and know
my anxious thoughts.

PSALM 139:23

Rejoice in the Lord always. I will say it again: Rejoice! Let your gentleness be evident to all. The Lord is near. Do not be anxious about anything, but in everything, by prayer and petition, with thanksgiving, present your requests to God. And the peace of God, which transcends all understanding, will guard your hearts and your minds in Christ Jesus.

Finally, brothers, whatever is true, whatever is noble, whatever is right, whatever is pure, whatever is lovely, whatever is admirable—if anything is excellent or praiseworthy—think about such things. Whatever you have learned or received or heard from me, or seen in me—put it into practice. And the God of peace will be with you.

PHILIPPIANS 4:4-9

My Strengths in Offering Hospitality

My Weaknesses in Offering Hospitality

Great Examples of
Hospitality and What I Learned from Them

My Plan to Grow in Offering Hospitality

• Notes •

· Notes ·

· Notes ·

· Notes ·

· Notes ·

· Notes ·

•Notes•

· Notes ·

Other Books Available from DPI

She Shall Be Called Woman, Volume 1
Old Testament Women
Edited by Sheila Jones and Linda Brumley

She Shall Be Called Woman, Volume 2
New Testament Women
Edited by Sheila Jones and Linda Brumley

Raising Awesome Kids in Troubled Times
By Sam and Geri Laing

Mind Change: The Overcomer's Handbook
By Thomas A. Jones

The Victory of Surrender
By Gordon Ferguson

The Disciple's Wedding
By Nancy Orr

Life to the Full
By Douglas Jacoby

For more information
on these books and many others call
1-800-727-8273

Or from outside the US call
1-617-938-7396